Discovering the Joy of Jesus

STONECROFT

HARVEST HOUSE PUI
EUGENE, OREGO

D0181070

Cover by Koechel Peterson & Associates, Inc., Minneapolis, Minnesota

Cover photo © iStockphoto / Thinkstock

DISCOVERING THE JOY OF JESUS
Stonecroft Bible Studies
Copyright © 2013 by Stonecroft Ministries, Inc.
Published by Harvest House Publishers
Eugene, Oregon 97402
www.harvesthousepublishers.com

ISBN 978-0-7369-5567-6 (pbk.)
ISBN 978-0-7369-5568-3 (eBook)

Printed in the United States of America

14 15 16 17 18 19 20 21 / VP-JH / 10 9 8 7 6 5 4 3

Contents

Acknowledgments

Stonecroft wishes to acknowledge and thank Janice Mayo Mathers for her dedication in serving the Lord through Stonecroft. Speaker, author, and member of the Board of Directors, Jan is the primary author of revised Stonecroft Bible Studies. We appreciate her love for God's Word and her love for people who need Him. Special thanks goes to the team who prayed for Jan, and those who edited, designed, and offered their creative input to make these studies accessible to all. Stonecroft is also grateful to Lucille Sollenberger, who is now with the Lord she loved and served, for the original development of this study.

Welcome to
Stonecroft Bible Studies!

I t doesn't matter where you've been or what you've done...God wants to be in relationship with you. And one place He tells you about Himself is in His Word—the Bible. Whether the Bible is familiar or new to you, its contents will transform your life and bring answers to your biggest questions.

Gather with people in your communities—women, men, couples, young and old alike—and find out together how the Bible's book of Philippians reveals joy, which is a quality of life that goes beyond everyday events and happenings, whether good or bad. You'll see how joy is closely connected with sharing the life of Jesus Christ.

Each chapter of *Discovering the Joy of Jesus* includes discussion questions to stir up meaningful conversation, specific Scripture verses to investigate, and time for prayer to connect with God and each other.

Discover more of God and His ways through this small-group exploration of the Bible.

Tips for Using This Study

This book has several features that make it easy to use and helpful for your life:

- The page number or numbers given after every Bible

reference are keyed to the page numbers in the *Abundant Life Bible*. This paperback Bible uses the New Living Translation, a translation in straightforward, up-to-date language. We encourage you to obtain a copy through your group leader or at stonecroft.org.

- Each chapter ends with a section called "Thoughts, Notes, and Prayer Requests." Use this space for notes or for thoughts that come to you during your group time or study, as well as prayer requests.

- In the back of the book you will find "Journal Pages"—a space available for writing down how the study is changing your life or any other personal thoughts, reactions, and reflections.

- Please make this book and study your own. We encourage you to use it and mark it in any way that helps you grow in your relationship with God!

If you find this study helpful, you may want to investigate other resources from Stonecroft. Please take a look at "Stonecroft Resources" in the back of the book or online at **stonecroft.org/store**.

stonecroft.org

Introduction

Happiness. It's what everyone seeks and seldom finds. The most outstanding quality of happiness seems to be its elusiveness—or its brevity. Perhaps it's because of a mistaken sense of what happiness consists of. Or maybe the expectations surrounding it are too high. Happiness is like an itchy spot in the middle of your back. It's just out of your reach, and no one else can quite scratch the right spot for you.

The good news is that there is a solution to the elusiveness of happiness. It's found in the book of Philippians. The author of the book is a man named Paul, who lived during the first century.

Saul—the name by which Paul was known during the first part of his life—was a well-educated, devout Jew who was also a Pharisee. Pharisees were a strict religious group that rigorously adhered to the Law of Moses (found in the first five books of the Old Testament) and the more than 600 other laws that religious leaders had tacked on down through the centuries.

Saul did not believe that Jesus was the Son of God. In fact, he actively sought out followers of Jesus in order to harass them, arrest them, and have them beaten or worse. Then one day, as he was traveling from Jerusalem to Damascus, he had a remarkable encounter with

Jesus, and his life was radically changed. You can read this remarkable story in Acts 9:1-19 (pages 837-838).

After his life-changing experience, Saul became known as Paul. And once Paul was convinced that Jesus was the Son of God, he became as committed to following Jesus as he had been to being a Pharisee. His entire life from that point on was devoted to telling others about the life-changing power of a personal relationship with Jesus Christ. He willingly turned his back on the life he had known in order to become a missionary, traveling continually to spread the Gospel.

His first journey as a missionary took him from Antioch, Syria to Cyprus and other cities in what is now Turkey. He was accompanied by a man named Barnabas. Wherever they traveled, they preached salvation through faith in Jesus Christ.

On Paul's second missionary journey, he and his companions visited groups of believers who had been converted on his first journey. They also traveled to Macedonia (the northern part of Greece), where the city of Philippi was located. The first church located in Europe was established there. Read Acts 16:11-15 (page 845) to learn about the first believers in that church.

The city of Philippi had been founded by King Philip II of Macedon, father of Alexander the Great. It was located about ten miles inland from the Aegean Sea and was in a strategic position on the Egnatian Way, the major east-west Roman highway through Macedonia. The city's greatest fame came in 42 BC, when Antony and Octavian (who later became Caesar Augustus) defeated Brutus and Cassius. As a result, Philippi became a Roman colony and obtained special privileges. The city's inhabitants consisted of Thracians, Greeks, Romans, and some Jews.

The book of Philippians is actually a letter Paul wrote to the Christians living in Philippi. It is perhaps the most personal of all Paul's letters to the various churches in existence then, and it revealed his strong personal attachment to the people of that church. They had strong affection for him as well, prayerfully and financially supporting his endeavors. As he wrote, Paul had only praise for them and thankfulness to God for this group of believers.

His purpose was to encourage them in the midst of the very challenging times they were experiencing. He wanted to instruct them on how to experience joy even in their difficulties. What is remarkable about this letter is that Paul was writing it from prison. He was experiencing his own extremely challenging circumstances, but you will not find sadness or discouragement in his words.

In this book Paul urges Christians to follow his example, showing us how we can experience a level of abiding joy that defies logic—a joy not at all dependent on our circumstances—as we embrace the transforming power of Jesus Christ. The study of Philippians can be life altering for you if you will open your heart to what God wants to teach you. I look forward to sharing the journey with you.

The Church of Philippi

Philippians 1:1-11

My uncle and aunt's relationship was a sterling example of what marriage was meant to be. As a young child I was drawn to their home, enchanted by the joy I felt there. As a teenager, I watched them closely, wanting to understand what was different about their relationship so I could find the same for myself when the time was right. As a young woman in love, I asked my aunt, who'd been married for some 30 years by then, "Do you still get excited when he holds your hand?" She assured me that she did.

As their sixty-fifth anniversary approached I asked her how they were going to celebrate. She told me it was their habit to always go to a new spot not too far away, since they weren't travelers. They always sought out a new place along the river near their home or a different meadow on a different mountain peak close by. Sometimes they'd go to a new cafe in a neighboring community, but they always found a different place. "This year," she said, "we'll celebrate right here on the front porch. We've never stayed home before, so this seems like a perfect place." She said this with authentic anticipation, ignoring the obvious point that the front porch was their only viable option because of my uncle's sharply declining health.

Not long afterward my uncle died, and my aunt was left to greet each day alone. Several months later she fell and broke her hip. I went to visit her at the nursing home where she was recuperating. In spite of her dreary surroundings and uncertain future, her eyes lit up when she saw me.

As we visited she told me about a day not long after my uncle's death when her grief grew so sharp it became a physical pain in her chest. She cried out, "Oh, Lord, comfort me!" She paused for a moment as she told me this, remembering. Then she smiled. "The pain has never come back!" she said. "Even through this, God has filled me with an unexplainable peace. I'm not worried about where I'll go from here or the finances or anything else, because He is with me, and I know I'll be okay."

As I left her room that day, I thought about the example she and my uncle had been for me throughout my life—not just of marriage, but of what a life committed to Jesus looks like. That's what had always inspired me: their shared, transforming faith in God that infused them with an abiding joy. I never saw that joy dim through all of the challenges of their lives.

✺

Prayer

Lord, I know I can be truly glad. There is wonderful joy ahead, even though I have to endure many trials for a little while. I love you even though I have never seen you. I trust you and rejoice with a glorious, inexpressible joy. You shine your light on me and fill me with joy when my heart is right. Because of you I will live in joy and peace (1 Peter 1:6,8, page 934; Psalm 97:11, page 458; and Isaiah 55:12a, page 561).

In his letter to the Philippians, the apostle Paul provides a powerful example of how we can have joy in every circumstance. In spite of all he endured—and we'll see soon that he endured a lot—nothing dimmed his passionate love for Jesus. It only made it fiercer.

Paul's Commitment

Paul began his letter in the custom of that time period by telling who wrote the letter and who the letter was addressed to. Read Philippians 1:1-2 (page 899).

In most of his letters to other churches Paul refers to himself as an apostle. An example of this is in Ephesians 1:1 (page 895).

How does Paul refer to himself in the beginning of Philippians?

Why do you think he referred to himself as a slave of Jesus Christ?

Paul's commitment to Jesus was wholehearted. He did not let the price Jesus had paid for him, which was dying on the cross for his sins, dim in his mind. From the time of his conversion, he no longer considered himself to be his own person. His gratitude led him to give himself fully to Jesus—heart, mind, and soul. Nothing changed that.

When have you felt a similar level of commitment to someone or some cause? How did that commitment level affect your actions?

Paul's ability to find joy in any circumstance was directly related to his total commitment to Jesus. As we study this book, I think you'll find Paul's example to be compelling.

Paul mentions another man, Timothy, in his greeting. Timothy was a younger co-worker, but his commitment to Jesus was just as strong. He accompanied Paul on missionary trips. Timothy had been with Paul when the church in Philippi was founded and had spent some time teaching and encouraging the church. The Christians in the city were well acquainted with both men.

Who is the letter addressed to?

Paul's letter embraces the whole congregation equally, and because of their commitment to God, he refers to them as being *"God's holy people." Holy* does not mean they were perfect. Rather, it means that as Christians they were set apart from the world through their trust in Christ as their Savior. Read the following passages and note what they say about living a holy life.

1 Peter 1:14-16 (page 934)

1 John 2:15-16 (page 942)

1 John 5:1-5 (page 943)

2 Corinthians 6:14-18 (page 885)

The Bible is the standard for our conduct. The character and nature of God fuels our Christian living. When we become a follower of Jesus, the Holy Spirit comes to dwell within us to enable us to live as God's holy people. Lives characterized by purity, power, and joy reflect God.

Ask God to teach you to do His will and to help you to live a holy life that pleases Him, a life that says, "Less of what I want, more of what you want—less of me, and more of your Holy Spirit working in me."

Grace and Peace from God

Verse 2 combines the general Grecian salutation of *"grace"* with the usual Hebrew greeting of *"peace."* It's a wonderful way to greet someone. Look at the salutation again: *"May God our Father and the Lord Jesus Christ give you grace and peace."*

How would you define *grace*?

Grace is used in the New Testament as the highest expression of the favor of God. It is God-given forgiveness that is undeserved. Paul is asking for all the favor of God for time and eternity to be given to his friends at Philippi!

How would you define *peace*?

One definition of *peace* is confident rest despite what is happening around us.

Read Romans 5:1 (page 860). How can we have peace with God?

Notice how Paul recognizes the oneness of the nature of God when he speaks of God our Father and the Lord Jesus Christ in the same sentence. Many other places in the Bible establish the unity of God the Father, God the Son, and God the Holy Spirit. Read the following verses for some examples of this:

John 17:11,21-23 (page 825)

John 15:26 (page 824)

John 16:15 (pages 824-825)

Partners with Paul in God's Work

Read Philippians 1:3-5 (page 899). How did the Philippians partner with Paul?

Even though Paul had not seen them for years, he thought of them often and thanked God for each one of them. He does not mention the opposition he ran into when he first visited their city or even his public beating and brief imprisonment (Acts 16:19-23, page 845). The very difficult circumstances that accompanied his visit meant nothing in comparison to the people who came to believe in Jesus while he was there.

As proof of how much he thought of the Philippians, Paul told the people that he always prayed for them with joy!

Is there someone you pray for with great joy? Why does it give you joy to pray for them?

In thinking about who I pray for with great joy, the first person who comes to mind is my daughter-in-law Lorena. When she became a believer I could not pray for her without smiling. Her hunger to learn all that she could challenged me to learn more. I love praying for her spiritual growth and am delighted as I see those prayers answered. I think that's why Paul so loved the Philippians. He saw their faith first bud out and then watched them bloom into fully devoted followers of Jesus, passionate about Christ as he was.

Thinking of the joy and gratitude Paul felt when he thought about the Philippians, is there someone who brings out a similar joy in you? Why?

We do not come in contact with a single person without leaving some influence on their life. Every word we speak and everything we do leaves a mark, good or bad. We need to consider what effect our lives have on those who see and know us.

In verse 5, Paul mentioned that the Philippians fully supported his work, carrying on in his absence the magnificent task of spreading the Gospel. Their passion for God did not fade away when Paul was no longer physically present with them. They were not dependent on him for their spiritual health. Their faith enabled them to stand strong even when they were enduring severe challenges. They continued to grow spiritually and continued to share the Good News with the people around them. No wonder Paul drew so much pleasure from thinking about them.

What are some ways we can help spread the Gospel today?

Prayer is always the starting place—asking God to give us courage and to make us aware of the opportunities around us. As we share our faith, we will find our own faith growing, and our passion to serve Jesus will soon become the motivating factor in all we do. Imagine the impact we could have on our world if we all became as committed as Paul and the Philippians were to following Jesus!

God's Work on Our Behalf

There is no doubt that a personal relationship with Jesus brings about a life transformation, but according to Philippians 1:6 (page 899), who actually does the transforming work?

God is the One who does the work, not us. Jesus' perfect life and death on the cross ensure that God sees us as pure and holy. However, we know by experience that we don't yet act perfectly pure and holy. We must become more like Jesus as we mature in our faith. God helps us become more like Him by changing our heart to want His will and our hands to do His will. And as we mature, He will put the opportunities to influence others in our path. He will put the words in our mouth and produce the results. Transformed lives are His department.

What will God do for us according to 1 Corinthians 1:8-9 (page 870)?

Contemplate for a moment the thought of being *"free from all blame."* In spite of everything we have done—the stupid mistakes, the foolish choices, the selfish actions—in spite of *everything*—we will be *"free from all blame"* when He returns. Christ took the blame, the sin, on Himself when, as the perfect sacrifice, He died on the cross. In God's eyes we are innocent and blameless.

Why do you think God would do this for us?

God is faithful to do what He says. One thing we can count on in this life is the fact that God is faithful. He keeps His promises. Not only is He faithful, He invites us to partner with Jesus! What an unbelievable, incomprehensible privilege to be partners with the One who died for our sins. We, the guilty, become partners with the innocent and are considered innocent through our relationship with Christ.

What does 1 John 3:2 (page 942) say about us?

What do parents do for their children?

One thing parents do as they raise their children is to prepare them for the future. That is what God is doing for us as His children. He is preparing us for the future—both our immediate future on the present earth and our eternal future with Him in the new earth and heaven. Every circumstance, experience, victory, failure, joy, and heartache is equipping us for our future. He is helping us to become more like Jesus.

Sharing God's Love

Read Philippians 1:7-8 (page 899).

Do you hear the sincere and tender affection in Paul's words? What makes his feelings for the Philippians so remarkable is that at one point in his life, Paul would not have had anything to do with them. They were Gentiles, and Jews and Gentiles did not mix. Paul was not only a Jew, he was also a Pharisee—one of the strictest sects of Judaism. His deep affection for the Philippians is one evidence of the remarkable transformation God brought about in his life.

What are some attitudes that God has transformed within you since you became a follower of Jesus?

What is the *"special favor of God"* that Paul says the Philippians share with him?

Paul's imprisonment was due to his work in spreading the Good News that salvation comes through Jesus Christ. The Philippians were enduring persecution for the same reason, but Paul does not see his imprisonment or their persecution as a negative, but rather as proof they were doing the right thing! He was *happy* to suffer for the cause of Jesus. It's a remarkable attitude—one that can keep discouragement and depression at bay. He elevates positive thinking to a whole new level.

How has this type of positive thinking affected your life in the past?

Look back over Philippians 1:3-8 and ask yourself the following questions:

- Do I pray for others who are followers of Jesus?
- Do I encourage them and show gratitude for their commitment?
- Do I cooperate with them in telling others about Jesus Christ?

Ask God to give you an opportunity to share His love with someone. Ask Him to give you courage to speak His truth.

Prayer for Others

In Philippians 1:9-11, what brings *"much glory and praise to God"*?

Paul's prayer was focused entirely on the Philippians' spiritual well-being. He did not pray that God would protect them from persecution or that He would provide for their physical needs. Instead he prayed that their love would continue to overflow in greater measure. What he asked for in verse 10 is especially important—that they would know *"what really matters."* Think about that for a moment.

If we are clear on what really matters and focus our attention on that, what difference will that make in how we live our lives?

Unfortunately, so much of our time and energy goes into other things. But when our focus is fixed on God's love for us and looking for opportunities to share that love, everything else will fall into a proper perspective. What tends to cause us stress will not be nearly so stressful.

Prayers are usually an expression of the deepest desires of the heart.

What subject occupies most of your prayer time? Physical needs such as finances, health, or a particular circumstance? What about emotional needs such relationship issues, loneliness, or unhappiness? What about the needs of family and friends?

Are the bulk of your prayers for your own needs or for others?

What if you started praying Paul's prayer for yourself, as well as for your family and friends? Let's experiment with it. Next week, every time you pray for anything, first pray Philippians 1:9-11. Write it on a card you can keep handy, or input it into your phone—and pray it throughout the day. Note any difference it has on how your days go, and we'll share the results at another point in our study.

Honoring God with Our Lives

As our love for Jesus grows, we want more and more to live in a way that honors Him. As we read His Word, our understanding and knowledge increases as truth is revealed by the Holy Spirit, which leads to quicker discernment between what's the right or wrong thing to do. Better discernment produces a life that is more blameless and pure, which results in the kind of fruitful life that honors God.

What kind of life honors God, according to the following verses?

1 Corinthians 10:31 (page 876)

Romans 12:1-2 (page 866)

Matthew 6:33 (page 738)

Matthew 11:29 (page 742)

1 Peter 4:11 (page 936)

How can we know that we bring God glory in our actions?

It isn't only *what* we actually do that honors God, but it's also *how* we do it. It depends on our attitude. Speaking to crowds of thousands, helping your neighbors repair their roof, fixing dinner for your family, or transplanting a heart. These all equally honor God if our heart is aligned with His.

―――――――― *Personal Reflection and Application* ――――――――

From this chapter,

I see…

I believe…

I will...

Prayer

    Father, help me focus on winning your approval, not the approval of people, because I know that if pleasing people is my goal, I am not your servant. I know what is most important— that Christ died for my sins, just as the Scriptures say. He was buried, and He was raised from the dead on the third day, just as the Scriptures say. So help me be very careful to obey all your commands, to love you and walk in all your ways, to hold firmly to you, and to serve you with all my heart and all my soul (Galatians 1:10, page 890; 1 Corinthians 15:3-4, page 879; and Joshua 22:5, page 184).

Thoughts, Notes, and Prayer Requests

_____

_____

_____

_____

_____

_____

_____

Joy in the Midst of Suffering

Philippians 1:12-30

The movie *Black Hawk Down* tells the story of a daring rescue mission led by Staff Sergeant Jeff Struecker in Mogadishu, Somalia. Struecker told the story personally at a Christian Leadership Alliance conference and described the events leading up to the rescue.

His team had just returned from one harrowing and deadly rescue mission that had claimed the life of one of his men. In spite of all the missions he had been on as an Army Ranger, this was the first time he had sensed he might not survive. When he finally got his troops back to base, it was to learn that a Black Hawk helicopter had gone down in the same very dangerous place they'd just escaped from. He was told to empty the Humvees and take his men back out on another rescue mission.

Struecker, a committed Christian, described the sickening dread he felt when given orders to go back. As he was cleaning the blood out of the Humvee he began to pray, overwhelmed by fear of what lay ahead for him and his men. As he prayed, he said a sudden, unexplainable peace flooded his soul. He realized that if he, by some miracle, survived the rescue mission, he'd go home to the loving arms of his wife and their new child. If he didn't survive, he'd go home to the loving arms of his heavenly Father. He realized that whatever happened that night, whether he lived or died, he could not lose. [1]

Father, I dare to hope when I remember that your faithful love never ends. Your mercies never cease. Great is your faithfulness; your mercies begin afresh each morning. I will not keep the good news of your justice hidden in my heart; I will talk about your faithfulness and saving power. I will tell everyone of your unfailing love and faithfulness (Lamentations 3:21-23, page 624, and Psalm 40:10, pages 431-432).

When you become a follower of Jesus, your perspective changes. You begin to view your circumstances differently. As you learn to put your confidence in God and as you experience the truth of His promises, you view the challenges and heartbreaks of life through a different filter.

Romans 8:28-29 (page 863) is just one example of how a relationship with God changes your perspective.

What does it say works together *"for the good of those who love God"*?

Everything! Good and bad, heartbreaking and thrilling, positive and negative—God is able to weave the circumstances of our life together for His good and ours.

God is not a genie in a bottle. He is the Creator of the Universe.

He doesn't work magic at our command, but He always works for the good of His loved ones—whether we feel it is good or not! He works for our best—through good times and bad. He is doing all that is necessary to ensure that we draw closer to Him and change to become like Him.

Seeing the Positive in Hard Times

Read Philippians 1:12-14 (page 899).

The apostle Paul had the rare ability to see the positive side in circumstances. Most of us, when we look back on a difficult time, may be able to see something good that came from it, but Paul found the positive while in the midst of the difficulties. He could do that because of his strong faith in God. This passage is a great example.

What is Paul saying here in verses 12-14?

What an incredible outlook! He is happy to be in prison because it is giving him a whole new audience to talk to about Jesus. He is happy because his circumstances are giving other believers greater confidence to speak openly about their faith in Jesus.

This is what Paul wants other believers to know—that they can develop the very same attitude that he has, which is an attitude that will enable them to see good while in the middle of suffering and to have joy in the middle of pain. Such an attitude comes from fixing our focus on Jesus and refusing to look in other directions.

When we become Jesus' follower we are not guaranteed smooth sailing. In fact, remember that God told Ananias to tell Paul that he would suffer as a result of becoming a Christian (Acts 9:13-16, page 838).

And that is exactly what happened. As opposition to Paul's boldly proclaimed belief in Jesus grew, it resulted in severe persecution. However, he saw it all as an opportunity to spread the Gospel. Wherever he was detained or imprisoned, he preached to his guards and to other prisoners. He saw it as an opportunity.

Maybe you are wondering what is actually meant by the terms *Gospel* or *Good News*. These terms are synonyms and describe how Jesus, God's Son, willingly left heaven to come live on earth with the limitations of a human body. He was tempted in all the ways we are tempted, but He never sinned, not even once. He was 100 percent innocent, yet He was crucified like a common criminal.

At any point Jesus could have put a stop to what was happening, but He didn't because of God's love for us—a love so huge He was willing to let His Son, Jesus, pay the price for our sins so we wouldn't have to. Three days after being put to death, Jesus came back to life. There were many witnesses to this, and you can read about it in 1 Corinthians 15:3-9 (page 879). But the Good News is that because Jesus lives, we can have a personal relationship with God now and be with Him for eternity after we die. That's the Gospel in a nutshell.

When you believe that Jesus is the Son of God who died for your sins, everything about your life changes. This is the most important decision you will ever make. For more information, see the "Know God" section on pages 147–149.

But just as Ananias told Paul he would suffer for his decision, the same is true for us today. There is a price to pay. Some people won't understand about your changed life; some may reject you. Read the following verses to see how we are called to respond to this.

1 Peter 2:21 (page 935)

1 Peter 4:16 (page 937)

Romans 8:18 (page 862)

1 Peter 5:10 (page 937)

No one likes the thought of suffering, but God has promised that He will be with us every day, even when we encounter suffering. His presence alone will *"restore, support, and strengthen you, and he will place you on a firm foundation"* (1 Peter 5:10, page 937). Though that does not make suffering easier, we can be assured that He will be with us in the midst of it, causing *"everything to work together for the good of those who love God and are called according to his purpose for them"* (Romans 8:28, page 863).

Attitudes and Motives

Read Philippians 1:15-20 (page 899).

Here again we see Paul's remarkable God-given attitude at work. He wasn't worried about those who were preaching about God with less than honorable motives. All that mattered to him was that the Gospel was being shared, even if it meant more suffering for him.

It is easy to get sidetracked by people, groups, or church denominations we don't agree with. We can worry about them, criticize their beliefs, or pass judgment on them, but the more our focus is on them, the less it is on God. When our focus is skewed, other things about us become skewed. That was the secret Paul had learned—to not let things or people pull his focus away from Jesus.

God protects His Word and sees to it that it bears fruit.

According to Isaiah 55:11 (page 561), what are the characteristics of God's Word?

The motives we should be concerned with are our own. What does Proverbs 16:2 (page 492) say?

We should closely examine the motives behind our actions. Are they clouded with an unhealthy sense of competition, jealousy, or ambition? Are we doing what we do for any reason other than glorifying God, bringing Him honor, or making Him look good to the people around us? If you struggle in this area, take some time to pray and ask God to adjust your attitude. Our true heart is revealed through our actions and attitude.

Paul's life philosophy is summed up in Acts 20:24 (page 849).

Whether in prison or free, facing life or death, Paul took every opportunity to proclaim the Gospel of Jesus Christ.

Paul wrote this letter to the Philippians while he was in prison. He did not know how his trial would turn out or what the future held for him, but he had decided that regardless of the outcome, his attitude and behavior would advance the Gospel. The desire of his heart was that he would always bring glory to God.

Have you experienced a difficult circumstance where you were determined to walk through it in a way that would glorify God? What was the outcome and how did people respond?

Being Christ-Centered

Read Philippians 1:20 (page 899).

Paul was fully committed to Jesus Christ. When he became a believer, he did a complete one-eighty. As a result of God's power at work in him, his impact on the world, even thousands of years later, is tremendous.

Read Philippians 1:21 (page 899).

What do you think Paul is saying here?

Whether we live or die, we cannot lose! Imagine how much more at peace we would be about everything—if we fully grasped the truth of what Paul is saying here. He continues his explanation in Philippians 1:22-26 (page 899).

Did you notice verses 24 and 25? Who was his focus on?

His focus was not on what he would like most, but rather on what would be best for the Christians he worked with.

This is the secret of Paul's joyful life: a Christ-centeredness that puts others first. Do you sense any hint of martyrdom in Paul's attitude? No—instead he sees whatever happens as part of the privilege of serving God.

The Privilege of Trusting God in Suffering

What are the instructions and encouragements Paul gives in Philippians 1:27-28 (page 899)?

What do you think Paul meant by *"live as citizens of heaven"*?

When we become followers of Jesus, our citizenship changes. We become children of God, joint heirs with Jesus. Read Romans 8:14-17 (page 862).

God adopts us as His children, and we become His beneficiaries! It is hard to grasp the depth of His love, which prompts such inconceivable generosity, but it is the reality of becoming a follower of Jesus. We are identified as God's children, and our inheritance is in heaven. All of our behavior should reflect that.

Paul's instruction in Philippians 1:28 is again all about developing the right attitude. He reminded the Philippians that as children of God, they didn't need to be intimidated by the people causing them such trouble, because ultimate power belongs to God.

Read Philippians 1:29-30 (page 899).

What are the two privileges we have as children of God?

Suffering and *privilege* are in the same sentence. How do you think suffering can be viewed as a privilege?

The prospect of suffering is not a pleasant one, but when seen as a gift of God's grace, as is faith, it can be seen as a privilege. Christians are not to seek out suffering, but when it comes, we are to accept it as a gift from God and treat it as any other gift from His hand. His grace enables us to offer our suffering for the cause of Christ.

The concept of suffering is not easy to contemplate. Becoming a child of God does not mean life will suddenly become good, perfect, and wonderful. Let's look at what Isaiah 43:2 (page 550) says.

These are comforting promises, aren't they? God is with us at all times, making sure we are not consumed by our pain.

I think my favorite verse in regard to suffering—especially suffering caused by other people—is found in Genesis. If you're not familiar with the remarkable story of Joseph, it is well worth reading when you have a little time. (See Genesis 37, 39–45, 47, and 50, pages 31-43.) In a nutshell, on three different occasions Joseph suffered betrayal, the worst being the betrayal of his own brothers. Through nearly 20 years of suffering, he chose to trust God, maintaining an attitude that protected him from becoming bitter or angry.

Like Paul, Joseph knew who was ultimately in control of his life. He trusted God with the outcome. This young man who became a slave in a foreign country and acquired an undeserved prison record while there, eventually rose in power to become the second most powerful person in that country. Think about that. From a foreign slave with a prison record to a leader of the country! Only God could bring about such circumstances.

Later, when Joseph reconciled with his brothers and they wondered how he could forgive them, his answer is one to remember when we are suffering. Read Genesis 50:20 (page 43).

We can absolutely trust God no matter what is happening—knowing He is aware of every person and circumstance.

It is important to note that not all suffering is a result of our commitment to Jesus. Some suffering is simply a result of living in this world. According to John 16:33 (page 825) and Ecclesiastes 7:14 (page 508), times of heartache and tragedy come to everyone, whether we believe in God or not. And some of our suffering is a result of our own bad choices. Regardless of the reason behind our suffering, God is present. He will comfort and help us.

Joy As Part of Our Growth

It is also important to understand that Paul's joyful attitude was made possible because of the ongoing work of Christ within him. This work is nurtured as we grow in our relationship with God. We must give it time. The work He does within us is a continuing work—it takes time and discipline. Read the following verses.

Acts 17:11 (page 846)

Matthew 7:24 (page 738)

James 4:7-8 (page 932)

Which of these disciplines need to be better developed in your life?

Take a moment right now, and ask God to help you with this. If you like, write a prayer out below.

In Philippians 1:30, the last verse of the chapter, Paul reminds his hearers that *"we are in this struggle together."* It's always encouraging to know we're not alone; and when we belong to Jesus, we are never alone. He has promised He will never fail or abandon us (Hebrews 13:5, page 928).

Personal Reflection and Application

From this chapter,

I see...

I believe...

I will...

Prayer

Lord, help me to live in a way that will always honor and please you. Produce every kind of good fruit in me. Help me grow as I learn to know you better and better. Strengthen me with your glorious power, so I will have all the endurance and patience I need. Fill me with joy and thankfulness, for you have enabled me to share in the inheritance that belongs to your people, who live in the light (Colossians 1:10-12, page 902).

—————— *Thoughts, Notes, and Prayer Requests* ——————

Joyful Attitudes

Philippians 2:1-11

The American Revolutionary War was brutal and hard fought. The fledgling United States battled a military twice its size in its struggle to establish independence from Britain. Stories of incredible human endurance and courage abound from this time in history as American soldiers, led by the great General George Washington, pushed through to victory. One story tells about a soldier on horseback who came across a group of fellow soldiers trying to move a heavy piece of timber. A corporal stood nearby giving them stern orders, but the timber was just too heavy for the men to move. The man on the horse asked the corporal, "Why don't you help them?"

"Me?" the man replied. "Why, I'm a corporal, sir!"

The man dismounted and began helping. With his added strength the soldiers were able to slide the timber into place. Job completed, the man climbed back on his horse and turning to the corporal, he said, "The next time you have a piece of timber for your men to handle, Corporal, send for the commander in chief." The man on the horse was General George Washington, who some years later became America's first president. [2]

Washington was one of the most important men of his time but he saw himself as a soldier, working for a cause too important to worry about the proprieties of rank when there was a job to be done. Part of Washington's remarkable success had to do with his attitude of humility. In this chapter we'll be looking at the importance of humility and the power this attitude can release into our lives.

∾

Prayer

Thank you, God, for making me right in your sight by faith. Now I have peace with you because of what Jesus Christ my Lord has done for me. Because of my faith, Christ has brought me into this place of undeserved privilege where I now stand. I confidently and joyfully look forward to sharing your glory. I know that I can rejoice when I run into problems and trials, because I know that they help me develop endurance. And endurance develops strength of character, and character strengthens my confident hope of salvation. And this hope will not lead to disappointment. I know how dearly you love me, because you have given me the Holy Spirit to fill my heart with your love (Romans 5:1-5, page 860).

Unity Among Christians

In the second chapter of Philippians (page 900), Paul begins by asking a series of four questions that lead into a heartfelt plea for unity among the followers of Jesus.

What are those questions?

What is his plea?

The Message paraphrase has the questions as statements, the same as in the original Greek:

> *If you've gotten anything at all out of following Christ, if his love has made any difference in your life, if being in a community of the Spirit means anything to you, if you have a heart, if you care—then do me a favor: Agree with each other...*

Could Paul be clearer? In return for all we receive from Jesus, getting along with each other is the least we can do. Unity with others is essential to a strong personal relationship with Jesus, a healthy relationship with other believers, and an accurate portrayal to the world of what it means to be a Christian. Unity was of great importance during Paul's time, and it is just as important today. Jesus does not give us the option—He just tells us to do it!

Paul's plea in verse 2 is actually an excellent definition of unity. It says that unity is *"agreeing wholeheartedly with each other, loving one another, and working together with one mind and purpose."* It sets a very high standard but only because unity is so very vital among believers, which is why Paul gives so much time to the subject.

How would you say Christians today are doing, as a whole, on the unity scale?

How are you personally doing on the unity scale?

After his plea for unity, Paul goes on to list the behaviors necessary for a spirit of unity. They are the behaviors Jesus exhibited while He lived on earth. Before we read them, list what you think the behaviors might be.

Now read Philippians 2:3-4 (page 900) and list the behaviors Paul mentions.

How many did you match up?

Are you surprised by the similarities in the qualities listed? If you had to sum them up in one word or phrase, what would it be?

Clearly, unity with others is a *big* deal to God! Why do you think it's so important?

Unity and Humility

Strong unity is vital for our individual well-being because of the tremendous support and encouragement we can draw from each other. If you look at verse 2 again, this is such an important issue that Paul repeats the same thing in three different ways: *agree wholeheartedly* (none of this "go along to get along" stuff—he's asking for enthusiastic unity); *love*; and *work together with one mind and purpose*! Do you see the picture of solidarity this paints? There is no room for ego, and verses 3 and 4 make that very clear.

How does Romans 15:1-2 (pages 867-868) relate to this topic?

The strong ones are to help the weaker ones. We all work together to help each other live in unity.

There is one phrase in Philippians 2:3 that deserves a closer look because it is so counter to our human nature and so essential to taking on the characteristics of Jesus: *"thinking of others as better than yourselves."*

What do you think about this instruction?

This idea is especially challenging when you consider the fact that it doesn't define "others." Without a more specific term, others can only mean *everyone*. We are to think of everyone as better than ourselves.

It seems an impossibly high standard, but just for a minute, imagine what life would look like if everyone lived with this attitude. Think of the difference it would make in marriages, families, businesses, and churches. Imagine the difference it would make in politics and in international relationships. It's mind-boggling when you think about the impact this one attitude alone would have if even just half our population practiced it, or even just one-fourth. And think about this: What if *you* all by yourself started putting this instruction into practice. What difference would it make in your sphere of influence?

Living in unity does not mean that we become one giant rubber stamp, agreeing willy-nilly with everything. A casual glance around this creation and we see that God is a God of variety. There are no two individuals exactly alike. He made us each unique, with different personalities, strengths, and weaknesses. No two minds will agree perfectly. But we can be of one mind in regard to unity without being identical. Even in the midst of a variety of opinions, there can still be unity when we learn to treat everyone with deference and respect, when we develop the ability to view others as Jesus views them—worthy of dying for.

The Selfless Life

Philippians 2:5-8 (page 900) explains the attitude Jesus had in regard to us and one we should develop.

Have you ever really stopped to think about the fact that Jesus was and is God? He lived in the splendor of heaven without limitations of any kind. He created this magnificent world; He created us! He knew exactly what He was doing when He chose to live within the restrictions of earth's atmosphere and the physical limitations of humanity. But He chose to do it anyway, because He loves us. For that reason, He was willing to limit the use of His divine privileges, and He entered our world, where He lived, died, and was resurrected.

Humility means to be free from the presence of pride and to be filled with a spirit of deference or submission. A truly humble person is one who is disciplined to God's will. Jesus set the example for us when He cried out to God while facing His excruciating death.

What was Jesus' desire, according to Mark 14:36 (page 776)?

In the humanity of His body He longed for another way, but He submitted Himself to do what was necessary for us to have a relationship with Him. We need to understand that Jesus was also fully God; at any time He could have stopped the terrible process, but He chose not to for our sake. There was nothing weak about that decision.

Read Romans 12:1-2 (page 866). Consider this phrase: *"God's will for you, which is good and pleasing and perfect."*

Oswald Chambers writes in *My Utmost for His Highest,*

> *Our Lord's teaching was always anti-self-realization. His purpose is not the development of a person—His purpose is to make a person exactly like Himself, and the Son of God is characterized by self-expenditure. If we believe in Jesus, it is not what we gain but what He pours through us that really counts. God's purpose is not simply to make us beautiful, plump grapes, but to make us grapes so that He may squeeze the sweetness out of us. Our spiritual life cannot be measured by success as the world measures it, but only by what God pours through us—and we cannot measure that at all.* [3]

Imagine God pouring sweetness into you and then squeezing it out onto your family, your co-workers, the grocery-store clerk—everyone you come in contact with. What impact would that have on the life of those around you?

To live such a selfless life is impossible on our own. It is only possible when we are in tune with the Holy Spirit. God does not expect us to do this alone. This is why His Spirit—the same powerful Spirit that raised Him from the dead—comes to live in us when we commit our lives to Him. Through His Spirit He teaches us, brings things to our minds, and gives us the desire and the ability to obey moment by moment. He gives us strength and stability through trying and difficult circumstances.

Then why do we fail? Why do we find it so hard to view others as better than ourselves? It's because of our divided focus. Our loyalty is divided between God and the world (James 4:8, page 932). This schism could dull our ears to His prompting, cause doubts to grow in our mind, and blind us to His help.

God Honors the Humble

Philippians 2:6-11 may have been a hymn of the early church. It parallels Old Testament references to Jesus in Isaiah 9:6 (page 523) and Isaiah 53 (page 559).

Now let's look at the result of Jesus' selflessness. Read Philippians 2:9-11 (page 900).

What did God do?

Verse 10 is actually a New Testament prophecy meaning that one day every person in *all the universe* will bow to Jesus Christ and openly acknowledge that He is Lord. Someday all doubt and disbelief will be removed from everyone's mind about whether or not there is a God. Everyone will recognize Jesus as Creator of the Universe and Lord over all, to the glory of God.

Read Romans 10:9 (page 864).

When we acknowledge that Jesus is Lord, we are aligning ourselves with Almighty God. His power will begin to flow through us, enabling us to live free of the debilitating attitudes and habits that limit our lives and rob us of the joy He makes available to us. And just as Jesus' attitude of humility elevated Him to the place of highest honor, we will be elevated as well.

Do you remember what is ours as a result of our commitment to God? Reread Romans 8:15-17 (page 862).

Personal Reflection and Application

From this chapter,

I see...

I believe...

I will...

Prayer

Lord, please help me be of one mind with fellow believers. Help me to sympathize with them and love them as brothers and sisters. Keep me tenderhearted, and give me a humble attitude. Let me make every effort to respond to your promises. Help me to supplement my faith with a generous provision of moral excellence, and in turn supplement that moral excellence with knowledge, and knowledge with self-control, and self-control with patient endurance, and patient endurance with godliness, and godliness with brotherly affection, and brotherly affection with love for everyone (1 Peter 3:8, page 936, and 2 Peter 1:5-7, page 938).

Thoughts, Notes, and Prayer Requests

4

Sharing Christian Joy

Philippians 2:12-30

Carolyn had been my friend and neighbor for years. She was a "cup half empty" kind of person, and I always felt the need to cheer her up. Then within the span of one year, she suffered unimaginable sorrow. Her 23-year-old daughter was killed in a car accident. A few months later her 19-year-old daughter died after a brief illness. Shortly after that her only remaining child was diagnosed with terminal cancer. She walked around in a stupor as her weight melted away and giant circles appeared beneath her eyes. "I don't know why God is punishing me," she mumbled one day, and I didn't know how to respond to her overwhelming grief. I hardly knew how to formulate prayers for her because her troubles were so huge.

Carolyn moved from our neighborhood not long after this, and I lost touch with her. Several years later I ran into her at a retreat where I was speaking. I scarcely recognized her! Her skin glowed and her eyes sparkled. "Carolyn!" I cried, hugging her tightly. "How are you? You look wonderful!"

"I *am* wonderful," she said and then she explained her transformation. "I stopped focusing on all I had lost and started focusing on God. It changed everything. It made me feel loved by Him instead of abandoned by Him." She said that the tighter she clung to God the more she felt His love, and gradually He replaced her sadness with an unexplainable joy—more than she'd ever experienced even before her children died. She went on to say, "I know now their deaths were not God's punishment, and although I don't understand, I know He loves me."

I ran into Carolyn several times after that, and she didn't lose her joyful glow. Her focus on God's love had permanently transformed her into a "cup overflowing" type of person.

⋙⋘

Prayer

Lord, I will take refuge in you and rejoice; I will sing joyful praises forever. Spread your protection over me so that I, who love your name, may be filled with joy. For you bless the godly, O Lord; you surround them with your shield of love. You satisfy me more than the richest feast. I will praise you with songs of joy. I lie awake thinking of you, meditating on you through the night. Because you are my helper, I sing for joy in the shadow of your wings (Psalm 5:11-12, page 416, and Psalm 63:5-7, page 441).

Working Out What God Has Put in Us

The last chapter we studied set a very high standard to live by— the same selfless, loving attitude that Jesus had. Such an attitude is so contrary to human nature that we can develop it only by fully surrendering our lives to God. This chapter we will be getting down to the challenge of putting such an attitude into practice, as Paul shows us how to live a surrendered life.

A key part of it is to continually be increasing our knowledge of the Bible. The more we saturate ourselves with God's Word, the more our lives will be transformed by what it says. Read Philippians 2:12-13 (page 900).

It's easier to do the right thing when you have someone physically near you who can teach and encourage you and help you stay on track. Paul understood this and wanted to make sure the Christians in Philippi continued to stay strong in their commitment to God even in his absence.

What are the two things he tells them to do?

Notice that it says to *"work hard to show the results of your salvation."* We don't have to work to be saved. Our salvation is a gift of God we do not have to earn; we just have to receive it. When we receive Jesus Christ as our Savior, God begins to change our lives. Working to show the results of our salvation means that we make these changes evident by the way we live.

It's easy to confuse these two concepts because it is difficult to accept that our salvation is free. Let's look at what the Bible says about this. Read the following verses and note what they say about salvation.

Galatians 2:16 (page 891)

Ephesians 2:8-10 (page 896)

Romans 4:4-5 (page 859)

The Bible makes it clear that our salvation cannot be earned by any of our good works. But it also makes it clear that our good works are important for another reason. What do the following verses say?

Matthew 5:16 (page 736)

Titus 2:7-8 (page 917)

James 4:17 (page 932)

What we say and do matters. Our behavior shows people the difference that a relationship with God makes, and we are rightly called hypocrites when we say we believe one thing and do not act out that belief in our lives. By living a life that acts on our beliefs, we are a testimony to what God has done in our lives. But always choosing to do the right things and think the right thoughts is not easy. That is why Philippians 2:13 is so wonderful.

What truth does this verse state?

What does 2 Peter 1:3 (page 938) add that is helpful?

What do you find encouraging about those passages?

Do you realize the incredible proof this is of God's love for you? He gives us the desire and the power to obey Him. In no way, under any circumstances, are we ever on our own in our relationship with God. He is always fully aware of our struggles and our weaknesses.

How does this truth impact you?

The Problem of Complaining and Arguing

Now let's read Philippians 2:14 (page 900).

I think we would probably be shocked if we started keeping track of how often words of complaint or argument come out of our mouths. It might be interesting to tape a chart to our refrigerator and put a checkmark on it each time we complain or argue.

Why do you think Paul found this important enough to caution against it? What effect does complaining and arguing have on us and those around us?

How do you feel internally when you argue or complain? It doesn't prompt a pleasant feeling, does it? How does it make the other person feel? Does it promote a positive response?

Does *anything* positive result from such words? Some suggest that venting can be therapeutic, and that might be true, but how does the person you are venting to feel? What has been accomplished by the release of negative words? Did the circumstance change by your venting, or are you the only one that feels better?

The question that needs to be answered is whether it is necessary to complain in order to correct a problem. Recently I watched a server at a restaurant pour a cup of coffee for the customer at the table next to me. The customer took a sip and shoved his cup away. "The coffee's cold," he snarled. The server apologized and went to get another pot.

His complaint was legitimate; no one likes cold coffee. But he could have easily remedied the situation by using kind words instead of negative words. Then he and the server would have both had better days. Instead, his whole focus was on the fact that the coffee didn't live up to his expectations—it was all about him.

Think back to the last thing you complained or argued about. How could you have approached it in a more positive way and still taken care of the object of your complaint?

Read 1 Peter 2:21-23 (page 935).
What a consistent example of righteousness Jesus set for us!

What does this passage say He did rather than retaliate?

Is there any greater wisdom than that? God can handle any situation if we'll just leave it in His hands. Can you think of a time when you wanted to retaliate or argue but instead left it in God's hands? What was the result of your decision?

Shining Like Stars for God

Read Philippians 2:14-16 (page 900).

According to verse 15, why are we not to complain or be argumentative?

When our son Tyler was a teenager he was backing out of a parking space at the grocery store and hit a car that was driving behind him. Sick with dread, he climbed out of the car and was hugely relieved to see a fish sign on the back of the bumper because he knew the driver would be nice. However, the driver jumped from the car shouting curses. She was not exactly shining like light in the darkness even though she was advertising herself as a Christian with the fish insignia. That's the kind of advertisement God can do without. To the driver's credit, she called that night to apologize for her outburst—but her "advertisement" had already been published.

God depends on Christians to shine a light of hope in the world. He wants our lives to accurately reflect the love of Jesus. When you listen to the news, see blatant immorality, hear about corruption in government, or feel all of the pain and hurt in the world caused by people, you cannot deny the growing darkness of our world. Now more than ever, Christians need to be a bold and courageous light to keep the darkness at bay.

The analogy of *"shining like bright lights"* is significant:

- A bright light illuminates dark places, making them safe to navigate. Other people should see Christians as a safe place to go to for help, a trustworthy resource for navigating life. They should see us as individuals they can trust, depend on, and confide in.

- Lights are used for warning—to show where the danger is. Christians should live in a way that commands respect so that people listen when we speak about the importance of following God.

- Lights are used for rescue. Christians should be living without compromise, so their lives illuminate clearly the way to eternal life.

- Lights are used to invite and to attract attention. A Christian's attitude and demeanor should be appealing and attract people to Jesus. There should be a recognizable and magnetic difference about us.

The truth is, in spite of how it seems, people are starving for God. They want desperately to be convinced there is a God and that there is more to life than what they are experiencing.

What are some things you can do to increase the power or appeal of your life?

A Relationship with Jesus

Maybe you don't fully understand how to have a relationship with Jesus or how to explain it to someone else. It's important to use the authority of the Bible when talking to someone about becoming a believer. The following verses are some good ones to use. They will also help answer questions you may have. As you read them, note what they say.

Romans 3:23 (page 859)

Sin is any attitude, thought, or action that separates us from God. Sin is anything that we think or do that is in direct disobedience to what we learn and read in Scripture. Sin interferes with us living lives that bring glory to God and reaching the full potential He placed within us.

Romans 6:23 (page 861)

Unless we accept the gift of eternal life that God offers us, we will spend eternity without Him.

Romans 5:8 (page 860)

Jesus' death paid the price for our sins. He died in our place!

2 Corinthians 5:21 (page 884)

Jesus took care of everything. Are you ready to begin a relationship with Him today?

Romans 5:1 (page 860)

Jesus bridged the gap that our sin created between us and God. Nothing stands between us anymore.

Romans 8:1 (page 862)

From this point on, God sees us as clean—as if we had never sinned. It's a brand new beginning!

Romans 8:38-39 (page 863)

This is the best part of all. Nothing will ever separate us from God. His love for us is unconditional and eternal.

You might find it helpful to write these references in the front of your Bible or input them into your smartphone so you can find them easily when you want to share them or review them. They are also wonderful verses to memorize.

Sharing your faith with another person often happens with the people right around you—your friends, co-workers, and family. Remember, God is the one who brought you together, so you can trust His timing and leading to direct you to share the Good News. As you share your lives, listen to the Holy Spirit, who will prompt you when to say something.

Prayer is another important concept of sharing our faith. If there is someone you'd like to talk to about a relationship with God, start by praying for them, asking God to give you an opportunity. In prayer you can ask God to prepare the heart of the person you're praying for. However, do not be discouraged if you don't get the results you are hoping for.

What does 1 Corinthians 15:58 (page 880) say?

How people respond is between them and God. As we read earlier, leave it in His hands. Your responsibility is to do what He asks you to do. Read Mark 16:15 (page 778).

As Christians, it is our responsibility to share the Gospel. We need to give the people around us accurate information about God and how to have a relationship with Him. We can do this both by living a consistent life based on biblical principles and by verbally sharing the Gospel. We are most effective when our words and our actions match.

Faithfulness in Good Times and Bad

Read Philippians 2:16-18 (page 900).

Paul encourages us to hold firmly to the Word of Life. What do you think he means by that?

You can hear his love for the Philippians and his pride in their faithfulness. Verse 17, however, brings us back to the reality Paul is living with. He doesn't know what the immediate future holds for him, whether he'll be released from prison or face death. Regardless of the outcome, he is choosing ahead of time to view it as an opportunity to further serve God.

He reminds these Christians that their faithfulness is an offering to God as well. The liquid offering that Paul talks about is a reference to an Old Testament practice that was common in the sacrificial system of some ancient cultures (Numbers 15:1-10, pages 117-118). He also refers to a liquid offering in 2 Timothy 4:6 (page 915).

Paul considered it a privilege to suffer for God. And he wants the

Philippians to see it the same way. Life or death—either way we win when our lives belong to God, and that is a reason to feel real joy.

Turn back to Philippians 2:19-24 (page 900).
Paul obviously loved and trusted Timothy. Timothy had proven himself to be a hard-working, trusted co-worker and a faithful follower of Jesus. To find out a little more about Timothy, read the following verses.

Acts 16:1-3 (pages 844-845)

1 Corinthians 4:17 (page 872)

1 Corinthians 16:10 (page 881)

How would you describe Timothy?

Read Philippians 2:25-30 (page 900).

Epaphroditus was another committed Christian beloved by both Paul and the Philippians. Like Paul, he was willing to risk his life in serving Jesus.

Verse 27 sneaks in a bit of insight into Paul's life. Did you happen to notice his reference to *"one sorrow after another"*? To some, his incredible attitude of joy in all circumstances may make it seem like he is not in touch with reality. Have you ever known a Christian whose cheerfulness just doesn't line up with what's going on?

I once asked an unbelieving friend how she would define "Christian." She replied, "Someone who doesn't have a correct view of reality."

How do you see Paul's outlook as being different from people who give a sugar-coated picture of what it means to have a relationship with God?

We need to be careful not to paint an unrealistically rosy picture of what it means to follow Jesus. Part of accurately reflecting Christ is having authentic, appropriate emotions. Verse 27 shows that Paul doesn't deny the sorrow he has experienced. He just does not allow those sorrows to take his focus off God. That's what gives Paul his strength to endure.

Chapter 2 of Philippians is all about accessing the strength of God so that we don't get pulled under by circumstances. Paul challenges us to set aside the attitudes and behaviors that trip us up so that we can support each other as we follow Jesus.

Do you remember Philippians 1:9 (page 899)? Are you remembering to pray that verse each day? Are you seeing a difference?

Personal Reflection and Application

From this chapter,

I see...

I believe...

I will...

✎

Prayer

Father, help me to be a light in my world—like a city on a hilltop that cannot be hidden. I know that no one lights a lamp and then puts it under a basket. Instead, they place it on a stand, where it gives light to everyone in the house. In the same way, let my good deeds shine out for all to see, so that everyone will praise you. Help me to be wise and shine as bright as the sky. Help me to lead many to righteousness, who will shine like the stars forever. Show me the way of life, granting me the joy of your presence and the pleasures of living with you forever (Matthew 5:14-16, page 736; Daniel 12:3, page 678; and Psalm 16:11, page 420).

Thoughts, Notes, and Prayer Requests

5

Joy in Christ's Righteousness

Philippians 3:1-11

The great violinist Itzhak Perlman was performing for a large audience in New York City. Suddenly, in the midst of his performance, one of the strings on his violin snapped. The break was so loud the entire audience heard it. Perlman stopped playing and looked at the broken string. He closed his eyes, took a moment to reflect, and then signaled the conductor to go on with the music.

Anyone who understands the violin knows that it is impossible to play a symphonic work with just three strings, but Perlman chose to continue his concert. He actually recomposed the music in his head as he played, inventing new fingering positions to accommodate the loss of the string.

The audience watched in awe, knowing they were witnessing a once-in-a-lifetime performance. When the piece was completed and the explosive applause had died down, Mr. Perlman smiled, wiped the sweat from his brow, and said, "You know, sometimes it is the artist's task to find out how much music you can still make with what you have left."

Perlman already knew about persevering through adversity. Polio had disabled him as a child, forcing him to go through life with leg braces and crutches. He refused to allow his physical challenge to interfere with his musical gift. [4] You might be thinking that you don't need the ability to walk in order to play a violin, and that's true, but everyone knows you need four strings—except for Perlman, who proved that night that the gift of music is internal. A true musician will not be stopped by the lack of an intact instrument.

When we surrender our heart to Jesus, a transformation takes place deep within us. The Holy Spirit's presence is in us and will help us through the crises of our lives. Amidst the broken strings of our lives, the Spirit will help us recompose our song, finding a fingering that will glorify God.

Prayer

This is the day that you have made, Lord, and I will rejoice and be glad in it. I pray that you, the source of hope, will fill me completely with joy and peace because I trust in you. Then I will overflow with confident hope through the power of the Holy Spirit. Yes, you have done amazing things for me! What joy! (Psalm 118:24, page 468; Romans 15:13, page 868; and Psalm 126:3, page 473).

Joy Guards Our Perspective

The second chapter of Philippians ended with what sounded like a conclusion. It seemed like Paul was wrapping up his thoughts and giving some final words of encouragement as he told the Philippians about Timothy and Epaphroditus who would soon be coming to them. In Philippians 3, Paul gives the Philippians a reminder. Read Philippians 3:1 (page 900).

"Whatever happens." It's possibly one of the greatest dichotomies of life: rejoicing in the midst of pain or sorrow. Yet there is power in such an attitude of joy. Paul practiced it when in prison, when being

beaten for his faith, when shipwrecked and facing death, and when friends betrayed him. Whatever was going on in his life, good or bad, he rejoiced in the Lord.

The power of the Holy Spirit strengthens us and helps us reach out to God and rejoice in the middle of our sorrows or despair. There is a special grace that is provided from God when we are in such desperate places.

> "One of the greatest acts of worship is keeping a good attitude in a bad situation."
>
> —*Mark Batterson*

Paul talks about this all-sufficient grace in 2 Corinthians 12:9 (page 888). When we feel weak, He strengthens us, and His power is made known to us—and to those around us. So, rejoicing in God safeguards your faith like nothing else will.

First Thessalonians 5:16-18 (page 907) says something similar to Philippians 3:1 but takes it a step further.

What are the three things it tells us to do?

1.

2.

3.

Notice that between joy and thankfulness is prayer. Prayer is essential to an attitude of joy and thankfulness, because it connects us to God, who in turn pours His joy into us. They all work together.

But why does it say we are to do these things?

That's the bottom line. It is God's will for us. And if that seems harsh, to expect us to be joyful in all circumstances, consider this: God is our Creator. He created us to experience the best kind of joy, and often that is in the middle of even the most difficult circumstances. When He says to always be joyful, it is for our good as well as His.

An attitude of joy and thankfulness keeps our focus on God and not on our circumstances, allowing the Holy Spirit to flow through us and fill us with right attitudes that please God. Read Galatians 5:22-23 (page 893).

Joy is the second thing it mentions, right after love. And look at all the other things. They all have to do with our interactions with others. As we are obedient to God, the Holy Spirit fills us with every kind of goodness that then overflows onto the people around us. That's what makes us shine like lights in the darkness.

Inner Transformation

Read Philippians 3:2-3 (page 900).

Jewish males were circumcised as a sign of the covenant between God and the Jewish nation. It reminded them of God's promises and their duties to Him. Paul reiterated that there is no act or good work we can do to become righteous. Jesus accomplished that for us when He died on the cross.

Paul was warning against the evil workers whose belief was bringing division in the church. They had taken the rite of circumcision that had religious significance to the Jews and turned it into a requirement for salvation. There are people doing the same sort of thing today. They take what some people consider significant—religious rites—and turn them into requirements for salvation. These people cause division and damage among followers of Jesus. The Bible warns us to be on guard against anyone who causes division and contention, whether maliciously or out of ignorance.

The critics of the early Christians saw how much the followers of Jesus loved each other. They couldn't argue against the difference they saw in their lives. Today there are still critics of Christianity. We should live in a way that removes any reason for them to not believe in Jesus Christ.

In Philippians 3:3 Paul talks about those who are *"truly circumcised."* To see what he means, read Romans 2:28-29 (page 858).

What is *"true circumcision"*?

It is a spiritual act, not a physical act. By God's grace, the spiritual act of believing that Jesus, God's Son, paid the price for our sins and turning our lives over to Him produces a radical transformation both in our physical behavior and in our mental outlook.

Read Romans 6:6 (page 861).

When we give up our will for God's will, sin loses its power over us and we can walk in a level of freedom and joy we have not imagined. Paul understands from experience how easy it is to get caught up in wrong thinking for all the right reasons. In Philippians 3:4-6 (page 900) he describes to them how falsely "righteous" he used to be.

List the different credentials that Paul (and his peers) once thought earned righteousness.

Paul had been circumcised when eight days old, which was what the Jewish law required. He was a pure-blooded citizen of Israel from the tribe of Benjamin. Saul, Israel's first king, was also from the tribe of Benjamin. Paul's human heritage was something to be proud of.

By Jewish standards, Paul had been ardently religious and righteous in conduct. He was so zealous that he persecuted Christians because he believed that Jesus was a heretic. Paul *thought* he was honoring God by getting rid of followers of Jesus. But he was very wrong in that belief. It is important to make sure that the beliefs we hold that determine our behavior are fully in line with what the Bible says. Do not trust what people tell you if they disagree with God's Word.

When Paul encountered Jesus that day on the road to Damascus, he encountered Truth, and it changed everything. Read Philippians 3:7-9 (pages 900-901).

How does he view his former belief system?

One reason why Paul became such an effective, influential follower of Christ is that he left his old way of life behind and embraced his new way of life. He experienced the transforming work of Jesus.

What are some things—behaviors, attitudes, philosophies—you are still holding on to that are making it hard for you to live as God wants?

Compromises can make our life complicated. Ask God to show you where your compromises or incorrect beliefs are. Then ask Him to help you eradicate them from your life.

What does Mark 8:36-37 (page 769) say about committing our lives to God?

Paul thought he was on his way to "gaining the whole world," but then he encountered Jesus Christ. Once Paul saw the truth, he rejected the fallacies of his belief system and fully embraced God's truth without reservation. He let go of his past and moved full speed ahead into the destiny God had planned for him.

Knowing Him

What is it that Paul wants to experience in Philippians 3:10-11 (page 901)?

The Amplified Bible states verse 10 this way:

> *[For my determined purpose is] that I may know Him [that I may progressively become more deeply and intimately acquainted with Him, perceiving and recognizing and understanding the wonders of His Person more strongly and more clearly], and that I may in that same way come to know the power outflowing from His resurrection [which it exerts over believers], and that I may so share His sufferings as to be continually transformed [in spirit into His likeness even] to His death.*

We become intimately acquainted with God by spending time with Him, studying His Word, and experiencing His faithfulness in the middle of difficult times. Knowledge of God is a progressive experience. It is an ongoing deepening awareness of Him and

His power working through us. We need to live a continual life of growth in Him.

> Read Hebrews 5:11-14 (page 922). What does Paul say about these believers?

As we study and apply God's Word to our lives, and as we continually rely on the Holy Spirit for guidance, our lives will grow and change. And this transformative work will reflect Christ to those around us.

If you find it is a constant struggle to do the right thing, ask God to strengthen you through the power of the Holy Spirit. Ask Him to transform and renew your thinking and life choices through His Word.

Maturing in Christ

> Take another look at Philippians 3:10-11 and list what we can do to become spiritually mature.

Let's take a closer look at each of these things. We've already talked about how we can *"know Christ,"* but what about the second item: *"experience the mighty power that raised him from the dead"*?

What do you think that means?

When we trust Jesus as our Savior we are, in essence, spiritually resurrected. We were destined for death, but Jesus died in our place. As a result we are given the power to walk in a whole new way of life. Paul longed to experience in his life, more and more, God's enabling him to have increasing victory over sin and continual development into the likeness of his Lord.

The resurrection of Jesus is the cornerstone of the Christian faith. It proves His power over sin, over death, and over Satan. The power of God is always at work in us as believers—whether we see it or not.

The third thing we can do is to *"suffer with Him."* What do you think this means?

Christians are those who have been called by God into partnership with His Son (1 Corinthians 1:9, page 870). Being in Christ involves sharing with Him in all things, including suffering for righteousness' sake.

> And the fourth is *"sharing in His death."* Any ideas what this might mean?

Christ's entire life pointed to the great climactic moment of dying as a perfect substitute for us. Paul knew he must abandon himself to the will of his Lord, and that meant self-emptying and humbling as Christ experienced.

What happened after Jesus was put to death and buried? He didn't stay dead, did He? Three days later He rose from the grave, and He is alive right this minute. We should live in the newness of life Jesus gives us.

It's exactly like Paul said in Philippians 1:21 (page 899). *"Living means living for Christ and dying is even better."*

We cannot possibly share completely in the sufferings of Christ, yet we know that part of our commitment to Him will involve suffering. Jesus said this. Paul said this. And other writers of the Bible said this. The comforting assurance we have is that Christ Himself suffered, and so He knows and understands. Because our suffering (this suffering that is part of our call) brings glory to His name, we can embrace it. We can see, as Paul shared in Philippians 1:7 (page 899), that the *"favor of God"* is shown through his imprisonment.

Are you noticing any difference in your outlook on life, a shifting in your attitude?

The thing you will discover about joy is that it multiplies. As you experience joy you'll feel your capacity for it enlarging. You will notice the people around you responding to your joy because it is infectious! If you have ever wondered what God's purpose for your life may be, you will love our next chapter!

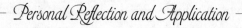

———— *Personal Reflection and Application* ————

From this chapter,

I see…

I believe…

I will…

Prayer

Lord, when I think of all this, I fall to my knees and pray to you, the Creator of everything in heaven and on earth. I pray that from your glorious, unlimited resources you will empower me with inner strength through your Spirit. Then you will make your home in my heart as I trust in you. May my roots grow down into your love and keep me strong. May I have the power to understand, as all God's people should, how wide, how long, how high, and how deep your love is. May I experience your love, though it is too great to understand fully. Then I will be made complete with all the fullness of life and power that comes from you (Ephesians 3:14-19, page 896).

Thoughts, Notes, and Prayer Requests

6

Joy in God's Will

Philippians 3:12-21

When our son Tyler was in fifth grade his teacher had the class memorize the preamble to the Declaration of Independence. I took his assignment very seriously, copying it on to several sets of three-by-five cards. One set I placed on his nightstand so we could review it before bed, one set on the dining-room table so we could work on it during mealtimes, and one set in the car so we could practice it while driving to and from school. By the time the assignment was due, anyone in our family could have quoted it perfectly.

The very next Sunday morning on our way to church, I opened my Bible and said, "Quick, Tye, let's memorize your Bible verse so you can get a piece of candy from the award jar." The minute the words left my lips I realized what I'd done. I had just taught my son that his school assignment, which had no eternal significance whatsoever, was more important than God's assignment to hide His Word in our heart so we won't sin (Psalm 119:11, page 468).

My mistake wasn't in teaching Tyler diligence with his school assignment—grades are important. But by treating his Bible verse assignment more casually, I was making the more important thing a less important thing. It's easy to inadvertently overemphasize the wrong goals, specifically the ones that don't have eternal significance. Paul had learned how to avoid this trap, and in this chapter he shares the secret.

Prayer

Father, I know that in a race everyone runs, but only one person gets the prize. Let me run to win! All athletes are disciplined in their training, doing it to win a prize that will fade away, but I want to do it for an eternal prize. Help me to run with purpose in every step. I do not want to just shadowbox. Help me to discipline my body like an athlete, training it to do what it should. (1 Corinthians 9:24-27, page 875).

Moving Forward in Your Faith

Paul's commitment to God, regardless of the personal cost to him, gave him confidence to use himself as an example of how to live in surrender to God. His resulting attitude of joy also provided an indisputable example of the benefits that accompany surrender. His desire was to only boast in what had made him weak and how Christ made him strong. Read 2 Corinthians 11:24-30, 12:9-10 (page 888).

These verses surely put Paul's commitment in clear perspective, don't they? He is a stellar example to us all of unflagging commitment. Now let's go back to where we left off. Read Philippians 3:12-14 (page 901).

Paul is not claiming to be perfect by any means, but he is pressing on toward that end. The word translated *perfect* means "to finish, to make complete." Paul's goal is to be complete in Jesus, achieving the full potential Jesus placed within him, which is to be an accurate reflection of Christ Himself. It's the same goal we should have for ourselves, pursuing it ardently by God's grace and enabling power, until we cross the finish line.

> Read Acts 9:15-16 (page 838) and note God's plan for Paul's life. (Remember that Paul went by the name Saul before his conversion.)
>
> What do you think God's purpose is for your life?
>
>
>
>
> Part of His purpose for you is found in John 15:16 (page 824).
>
>
>
>
> What do you think would define *"lasting fruit"*?

It's a good idea to examine our lives occasionally to see how much of our time is being spent on producing lasting fruit. Read the following verses and note what we can do to stay on track with God's goal for our lives.

2 Timothy 2:21-22 (page 915)

John 15:4-5 (page 824)

Hebrews 12:1-2 (page 927)

The first two passages show the importance of staying connected to God, which is what keeps us pure and honorable, a worthy example of what it means to be a follower of Jesus. The last passage tells us exactly how to live honorably and be a faithful follower of Christ.

What are the three specific instructions it gives us?

1.

2.

3.

What kinds of things slow you down from following Christ?

Often it's an ingrained attitude that trips us up, such as negative thinking or insecurity. Such attitudes hold us back from what God wants us to do. Sometimes it's habits such as procrastination or disorganization. Sometimes it's a behavior such as laziness or even overcommitment. It is especially easy to get caught up doing so many good things that the important things don't get our best. D.L. Moody, founder of Moody Bible Institute and one of the great evangelists of America, struggled with overcommitment. Before the disastrous Chicago fire of 1871 he was involved in Sunday-school promotion, YMCA work, evangelistic meetings, and other worthy activities. But after the fire, God refined his focus, and he devoted himself almost exclusively to evangelism. As a result thousands of people heard the Gospel. [5]

Whatever it is that keeps tripping you up, the solution is in the third instruction. *Keep your eyes on Jesus!* If you've ever watched runners in a race, they are looking only in one direction—the finish line. They do not glance behind to judge how they're doing in comparison to their competitors, and they don't glance to the side. Their focus is fixed on the finish line because they know it will cost them if they lose that focus.

Roger Bannister, a world-class athlete of the 1950s, became the first man in recorded history to run a mile in less than four minutes. Within two months, another runner, John Landy, had beaten his record by 1.4 seconds. Later that year, the two men met for a historic race. Landy held the lead as they started the last lap and it looked as if he would be the victor. As he neared the finish line, however, he risked a glance back toward Bannister and it cost him the race. "If I hadn't looked back," Landy later told a journalist, "I would have won!"[6]

Fix your eyes on God. Don't let anything distract you from the finish line ahead where Jesus is cheering you on.

Single-Minded Pursuit

Back in Philippians 3:13-14 (page 901), Paul shares the secret to the success of his single-minded pursuit of the goal.

What are three things he does?
1.

Oh that can be so hard, can't it? *"Forgetting the past"* means letting go of all that has hurt you. It means letting go of all your own mistakes and poor choices. It means letting go of things that happened over which you had no control. Letting go of the past means making the decision to not let it influence your life in any way, any longer.

What are the things you can't let go of? What keeps popping up in your mind at random times and interfering with your present life? Write them out below and then hold them out to God. Ask Him to destroy the power they have over you. Ask Him to give you an unobstructed view of Him to fix your eyes on. Living in the past destroys your future.

Now, what is the second thing Paul does?
2.

"Looking forward" is key. Coaches in all areas of our life say the same thing: Clearly defined short-term and long-term goals are essential to success.

What does your relationship with God mean to you? What are the things you will do in the short term to strengthen your relationship? What adjustments do you need to make? Write them out below.

What is the third thing Paul does?

3.

"Press on" is the challenge, isn't it? To keep putting one foot in front of the other when you desperately want to throw in the towel. To refuse to let discouragement or disappointment sidetrack you or slow you down. It is so worth it! Keep in clear focus that incredible heavenly prize that will be beyond our wildest dreams. God has promised to enable and reward our endurance.

God's desire, His goal for all His followers, is that we live our lives in full obedience and commitment to Him, accurately reflecting the heart of Jesus in every thought, emotion, word, and action. But He also has individual goals for us. For some it may be an ongoing, lifelong plan. For others His plan might change as we enter into new seasons.

Do you have a clear vision of what God's plan is for you during this season of your life? If you do, take some time to consider what things might be distracting you from fulfilling His purpose. Jot them down below along with some possible solutions to the distraction.

If you don't have a clear vision of God's plan, ask Him to make it clear to you. As you read the Bible and communicate with Him, He will guide you in the direction He wants you to go. Read Philippians 3:15-16 (page 901). The ability to persevere and maintain a godly focus comes with our spiritual maturity. Paul is encouraging the Philippians to keep progressing. And for those who do not see the need for such total commitment, God will keep drawing them toward that direction. Don't let others distract you from your own commitment. Like a runner in a race, keep your eye on the finish line and God will reward you.

Being a Worthy Example

Read Philippians 3:17-19 (page 901).

As we already mentioned, Paul is not putting himself on a pedestal, saying, "Look at me!" He is honestly asking the Philippians to follow him.

Whose example in your life do you follow? Why?

I became involved with Stonecroft Ministries because of a Bible-study teacher who invited me to one of their events. I was already a Christian, but I had great admiration for the way this woman followed Jesus and wanted to know what she was involved in. I had watched her go through various circumstances, coming to the right conclusions and making honorable decisions. It was how I wanted to live my life, so I accepted her invitation.

In what ways are you living a life that is worthy of being
followed?

Philippians 3:18-19 (page 901) describes people whose lives
are not worthy of following. Sadly, the implication in verse 18 is
that these people profess to be followers of Jesus but their behavior
proves otherwise.

What does verse 19 say they are headed for?

No wonder Paul said, *"I say it again with tears in my eyes..."* It is
a consequence of horrifying proportions and one that he is desperate for them to avoid. If we are not compelled by the same despera-
tion, we should ask God to keep the reality of hell in front of us so
that we will be passionate about telling others about Jesus.

What three characteristics do these people exhibit in verse 19?

1.

What do you think Paul means when he says, *"their god is their appetite"*?

This could be summed up in one word: self-indulgent. Their first and last thought is for themselves and they are never satisfied. This is the antithesis of Paul's example of self-sacrifice.

2.

Have you ever known a Christian who loves to talk about their wild past? They show no sorrow for how they once lived. Or have you found yourself in conversations where the participants veered way off course into topics that did not glorify God? How did you handle the situation?

3.

This part of life we're in right now is all we know. Eternity seems far removed, and for some of us, hard to imagine or grasp. So to live with our eyes on eternity is a challenge. But it is so important that we understand this life on earth is only a speck in the whole scope of time. Our perspective, our filter for everything we do, should be eternity.

Living in Light of Our Destination

Although we are living on earth, where is our true citizenship, according to Philippians 3:20 (page 901)?

Even though this life is all we know, it is not all there is. God has so much more waiting for us in heaven if we have accepted the life He offers us through His Son, Jesus.

Read Colossians 3:1-4 (page 903). What does it tell us to do?

Set our sights on heaven. Think about heaven. Focus on God who is waiting for us there. Anticipate the arrival of Jesus who will take us there. When you get bogged down with the realities of life on this earth, *stop!* Take a deep breath and turn your thoughts toward home— your forever home where there will be no realities that bog you down.
Read 1 Thessalonians 4:13-18 (page 906).

This is true reality—that Jesus is coming back to escort His followers to our real home in heaven where we will live forever with Him. To discover the truly wonderful aspect of this, read Philippians 3:21.

Oh, just imagine this: These earthly bodies that cause us so much distress will be changed.

Imagine for a moment. What might having our glorious bodies involve?

Whatever it means, our bodies will at last be like Jesus. Just as we now strive with God's help to have the attitude Jesus had, someday we will no longer have to strive. Instead, we will *"reach the end of the race and receive the heavenly prize for which God, through Christ Jesus, is calling us"* (Philippians 3:14, page 901).

As we finish this chapter, consider these questions:

If you knew for certain that Jesus Christ was coming back in one month, what changes would you make in your life?

Who would be the first five people you would tell about Jesus?

Ask God to give you the opportunity and courage to talk to those people.

——————— *Personal Reflection and Application* ———————

From this chapter,

I see...

I believe...

I will...

Prayer

Father, I am looking forward with hope to that wonderful day when the glory of our great God and Savior, Jesus Christ, will be revealed. I am looking forward to the new heavens and new earth you have promised, a world filled with your righteousness. As I wait for these things to happen, help me make every effort to be found living a peaceful life that is pure and blameless in your sight. And give me courage to tell others about you because I know you do not want anyone to be destroyed, but want everyone to repent (Titus 2:13, pages 917-918, and 2 Peter 3:13-14,9b, page 939).

Thoughts, Notes, and Prayer Requests

_____

_____

_____

_____

_____

_____

_____

_____

_____

_____

_____

_____

7

Peace and Joy in Christ

Philippians 4:1-9

In her book *It's My Turn*, Ruth Bell Graham wrote about waking up at 3:00 a.m. one night overwhelmed by the need to pray for a particular person. But in the darkness of those early morning hours her mind ran wild with "fears that only a mother can understand." Suddenly she sensed God saying to her, "Quit studying the problems and start studying the promises."

She turned on the light, opened her Bible, and read Philippians 4:6-7 (page 901). As she read these verses she realized the missing ingredient in her prayers was thanksgiving. She started to worship God and thank Him for the person she'd been praying for. She even thanked Him for the difficult spots of life that had taught her so much. As she prayed she said it was "as if suddenly someone turned on the lights in my mind and heart, and the little fears and worries which, like mice and cockroaches, had been nibbling away in the darkness, suddenly scuttled for cover." Worship and worry cannot live in the same heart; they are mutually exclusive. [7]

Prayer

Lord, I give my burdens to you, and you will take care of me. You will not permit me to slip and fall. I know you are always with me. I will not be shaken, for you are right beside me. Guard me as you would guard your own eyes. Hide me in the shadow of your wings (Psalm 55:22, page 438; Psalm 16:8, page 420; and Psalm 17:8, page 420).

You are going to love this fourth chapter of Philippians. It is filled with wonderful, practical helps for living a joyful life. Let's begin by reading Philippians 4:1 (page 901).

Paul's love for the Philippians is very evident. Their faithfulness to God fills him with joy and he views them as his crown, or reward, for all his hard work. How wonderful it must have been for these Christians to hear these words from him and to know he saw them as his crown.

Is there someone in your life who you view as your crown? Why?

Why might someone view you as their crown?

It's interesting to think about the impact our faithfulness can have on someone else's life. It shows how important our close walk with God is, not just for our own benefit but for the benefit of others following us.

Encouragement to Stand Firm

Philippians chapter 3 talked about the all-sufficient power of God, our heavenly citizenship, and the return of Jesus. Paul begins chapter 4 by saying in essence, "Therefore, because of these things, let's get down to business."

> What is the very first thing he tells the Philippians to do in verse 1?

This is an instruction Paul repeated in letters he wrote to other believers. In addition to *"stay true to the Lord,"* he gave them other instructions. As you read the following verses, make a list of his instructions, noting the number of times they are repeated.

1 Corinthians 15:58 (page 880)

1 Corinthians 16:13 (page 881)

Ephesians 6:11 (page 898)

2 Thessalonians 2:15 (page 908)

He uses *strong* three times and *stand firm* twice, plus *immovable*. Did you also notice the instruction to *"work enthusiastically"*? Why do you think he told them to be enthusiastic?

Another reason could be that it is much easier to stand firm about something for which you have great enthusiasm. The two mesh together for greater effectiveness.

In 1 Corinthians 15:58 Paul added a word of encouragement. What was it? How does knowing this encourage you?

Making Peace and Fostering Unity

In Philippians 4:2-3 (page 901) we catch a glimpse into the human side of life in Philippi.

What was it?

We don't know what the disagreement between these two women was about, but it had enough of an impact on the church that word of their dispute reached Paul in prison. These are clearly good women and strong believers, who had worked hard beside Paul to tell people about Jesus. Their heart was in the right place, but something caused their focus to drop momentarily away from God and onto themselves.

Have you ever been caught up in a conflict that you just couldn't seem to let go of? How did you ultimately resolve it?

We are human. In spite of our best efforts, we can find ourselves at odds with another person and a damaged or fully broken relationship between us. However, there is absolutely no excuse to continue to be part of the conflict. It can be the most difficult thing in the world to back down when you are convinced the other person is in the wrong, but it may be the right thing to do. To let a conflict continue resolves nothing and hurts everyone around you. It does not glorify God in any way.

Paul is gentle in how he addresses the issue, not taking sides and not criticizing their behavior, but appealing to them to resolve their dispute even as he commends their dedication to spreading the Gospel. Although we don't know who it was, Paul also employed the help of a "peacemaker," someone he trusted to help the two women find resolution.

Have you ever been in a position of peacemaker? What were the steps you took to bring about reconciliation?

Our world is in need of peacemakers. *Christians* need peacemakers! What does the Bible say about people who fulfill this role in Matthew 5:9 (page 736)?

There are two key attributes to being a peacemaker. Read Matthew 22:37-39 (page 753) and note what they are.

But this is the important thing to note: This is not a requirement *just for peacemakers*—it is a requirement for all who are following Jesus. This is a commandment God gave to us all. While it's true that some people have a gift for being peacemakers, God wants each of us to go through life as peacemakers—loving Him and loving people.

What does James 3:17 (page 931) say?

The wisdom that we get from God will always meet those standards. This does not mean we let things that are wrong go unconfronted. The Bible tells us to hold each other accountable. Read Galatians 6:1-2 (pages 893-894).

Paul was gentle and humble in his approach to the two women, treating them with respect, just as this verse tells us to do. Before we confront wrongful behavior, remember to first make sure you do not have the same issue (Matthew 7:1-5, page 738). When we are critical and unloving, we dishonor God and come across in a negative light personally.

As we discussed in chapter 3, "Joyful Attitudes," the Bible speaks clearly about the importance of unity among believers. Read the following verses:

1 Corinthians 1:10 (page 870)

Galatians 3:28 (page 892)

Ephesians 4:3 (page 897)

How do these verses show the importance God places on unity among believers? As we consider just how essential unity is, what can we do, in our sphere of influence, to contribute to a spirit of unity among believers?

Joy Makes Us Different

Read Philippians 4:4 (page 901).

Paul wants believers to access the joy that is available to them through their relationship with God. While we cannot rejoice over some circumstances we have to face, we can always rejoice that we belong to God, who holds those circumstances in His hands. Read the following verses to see what Jesus had to say about joy.

John 17:13 (page 825)

John 15:11 (page 824)

What Jesus wanted people to know was that having a relationship with Him would result in a level of joy that circumstances could not dim.

There is no denying that sometimes excruciating, terrifying circumstances drench us with worry and fear. Sometimes heart-wrenching loss knocks us to our knees and flattens us with grief. Sometimes an outrageous injustice slams into us and knocks us over with bitterness. To deny that a follower of Jesus would experience such emotions is to deny reality. But if our focus is on God and not on what has happened, we will not get lost in those emotions. He will help us through them so we become more connected to Him. It is this knowledge that is the wellspring of joy for a believer.

In Philippians 4:5 (page 901) what is another instruction Paul gives?

Again, Paul is encouraging us to be careful, even intentional, about how we treat people around us. Our treatment of others is one more way that Christ is revealed in us. John put it this way: *"Your love for one another will prove to the world that you are my disciples"* (John 13:35, page 823).

Gratefulness and Prayer Replace Worry

Read Philippians 4:6-7 (page 901). These two verses are so very powerful!

Verse 6 tells us four things to do. What are they?

1.

2.

3.

4.

It sounds simple: *"Don't worry about anything, instead pray about everything."* We all know it's not. But why isn't it simple? Why is it so difficult to pray and let go of our worries? It comes back once again to our focus. As long as we focus more on what is worrying us than we do on God, our prayers will do nothing to calm our worries—or even solve our problem. We can tell Him what we need all day long.

One key is in the fourth instruction: *"Thank Him for all He has done."* That is what will reverse the process. Thanking God for all He has done automatically switches your focus to Him!

It really is simple. God will help you with the needed discipline and determination. The minute a worry enters your mind, replace it with thankfulness for something He has done for you. This will keep pulling your focus away from the circumstance that is distressing you and fixing it on Him. The more you do this, the more natural it will become. As you do this you will begin to experience the result of these four steps as it is described in verse 7.

What will we experience?

Did you catch it? Not just God's peace, but a peace that *"exceeds anything we can understand."* It's a peace that cannot be explained, but it is absolutely real. As that peace settles down around your soul, it will put a guard around your heart and mind that will protect you from debilitating worry.

Nothing is too small for God to notice, and nothing is too great for Him to manage.

Read Isaiah 26:3 (page 535).

There it is again—the same promise in the Old Testament, written hundreds of years before Paul wrote his letter. Fix your thoughts on God and you will experience His perfect peace!

A Treasury of Good Things

Now we come to Paul's final instruction to the Philippians, delivered in the same warm and affectionate tone. Read Philippians 4:8-9 (page 901).

Often in this letter, Paul repeats the importance of both attitude and action.

In verse 8, what word does he use in telling us what to do with our thoughts?

Some synonyms for the word *"fix"* are glue, secure, or fasten. There is no space between two items glued together. In other words, glue your thoughts to good things, so there is no room for worry, doubt, or fear to squeeze in between.

The action part of his advice is in verse 9: *"keep putting into practice."* Here again his choice of words is important. He doesn't say put into practice. He says *keep* putting into practice. The way of life he is teaching them needs to become a continual, ongoing action in every season of life. He wants them to experience the incredible reality of a follower of Jesus. It is not a formal, dry, ritualistic show of religion. It is a vital, living, dynamic, relevant way of life.

God tells us that how we think determines how we act. Read Proverbs 4:23 (page 483).

If we guard our heart from unhealthy thoughts we will not get caught up in unhealthy behavior. If we fix our hearts on what is good and pure, our behavior will reflect that. It will be easier to follow God.

What does Matthew 12:35 (page 743) say?

Don't you love the phrase, *"treasury of a good heart"*? I want my heart to be a treasury of good, honorable thoughts, don't you? The truth is we need to give God control over what kind of treasury our heart will be. When a negative thought flits through our mind, it should not take root. Replace it immediately with a good thought. An effective tool for thought replacement is to use a memorized Bible verse. The minute a wrong thought appears, repeat the Bible verse.

Remember Philippians 1:9-10 (page 899), which we talked about in our first chapter? *"I pray that your love will overflow more and more, and that you will keep on growing in knowledge and understanding. For*

I want you to understand what really matters, so that you may live pure and blameless lives until the day of Christ's return."

Have you been reading that each day, and has it had any effect?

I copied the verses onto a card and have it by my computer. I read it over several times a day. The first phrase is the one I repeat to replace wrong thoughts that come to mind, and it is having a powerful effect on my thought process. For example, my mother-in-law, who lives with us, suffers from advanced Alzheimer's. Keeping good, pure thoughts in my mind can be a huge challenge some days. However, by repeating the prayer phrase "let my love overflow more and more," my thoughts are instantly commandeered to a higher standard, so God can change my words and behavior. His Word is not static. It is alive and powerful and life-changing.

"Preparation is half the battle" according to Don Quixote, so let's have a little fun preparing our minds for battle.

The following list has things Paul says in Philippians 4:8 to glue our mind to. Beside each item write several things that qualify. This will keep you prepared with some replacement topics.

Things that are true

Things that are honorable

Things that are right

Things that are pure

Things that are lovely

Things that are admirable

Things that are excellent

Things that are worthy of praise

Do you feel better just from thinking of things to write down? See the power in deliberately focusing our thoughts on good things? Ask God to help you control your thoughts. What a great way to end this chapter!

———— *Personal Reflection and Application* ————

From this chapter,

I see...

I believe…

I will…

❧

Prayer

God, please destroy every proud obstacle in my life that keeps people from knowing you through me. Capture my rebellious thoughts and teach me to obey Christ. May the words of my mouth and the meditation of my heart be pleasing to you, O LORD, my rock and my redeemer (2 Corinthians 10:5, page 887, and Psalm 19:14, page 422).

─── *Thoughts, Notes, and Prayer Requests* ───

8

Joy in Christ's Strength

Philippians 4:10-23

Before either of us was married, my cousin and I spent a year as missionaries in Micronesia. We home-schooled the five children of the missionaries living there and taught in the high school they ran for the islanders. It was a remarkable year of discovering how abundantly God keeps His promises. We lived exclusively by faith since, as volunteers, we weren't paid for our work. Neither did we raise funds ahead of time or send out letters for support while there. To up the ante, we'd only bought one-way tickets, trusting we'd have money for the return trip when our year was up.

Meanwhile, back at home, we had an aunt and uncle who were committed followers of Jesus. They lived very frugally on a limited income as they raised two little boys and helped pastor a tiny church in their small community. They decided my cousin and I were a perfect opportunity to teach their boys about missions. Each week the boys pulled their little red wagon along the highway, collecting pop cans that they converted to money and sent to "their missionaries." Now, a nickel a can doesn't seem like it would go very far in supporting two missionaries, but it is amazing how God can multiply a nickel!

Watching God supply our every need (Philippians 4:19, page 901) was breathtaking. Never once did we go hungry, and never once did we rely on the missionaries to feed us. Although sometimes what we needed arrived literally at the last minute, *abundantly* is the only word that describes how God took care of us. We sent letters to our aunt and uncle describing all the blessings we were receiving from their support, and they sent letters describing how God was blessing them. It was an amazing cycle of blessings, all coming from the hand of God just as He promised. The fun ending to this story was that we arrived in Micronesia with $300 between us, and one year later we arrived home with $300 between us!

Prayer

Lord Jesus, you have told me not to worry about everyday life—whether I have enough food to eat or enough clothes to wear. You tell me to look at the ravens that don't plant or harvest or store food in barns because you feed them. I know that I am far more valuable to you than any birds! All of my worries will not add a single moment to my life, so if worry can't accomplish a little thing like that, what's the use of worrying over bigger things? If you care so wonderfully for flowers, which are here today and thrown into the fire tomorrow, you will certainly care for me. I don't need to be concerned about what to eat and what to drink. I don't need to worry about these things because you already know my needs. Help me, Lord, to seek you above all else, and you will give me everything I need. I won't be afraid because it gives you great happiness to do this (Luke 12:22-26,28-32, page 795).

Years of imprisonment had kept Paul separated from the Philippians, and as we read his letter to them we can hear his longing to see them again. But we can also hear his pride in how strong their commitment to God remains. Above all we hear his passionate love for God that even his imprisonment does not dim. Now in this final chapter Paul lets the Philippians know how he is doing, assuring them that because of his relationship with God he is experiencing joy even in his challenging circumstances. He reiterates his appreciation for their continued support and reminds them of his love. Throughout everything he says he continues to weave caring instructions for them, using himself as an example.

Life-Changing Contentment

Read Philippians 4:10-12 (page 901).

This is an amazing couple of verses, a powerful example of how we can experience joy in all circumstances. Keep in mind again as we talk about this that Paul is in prison when he says that he has never been in need.

What did he say was the reason for this?

What a life-changing lesson he had learned! Paul was speaking from a wide variety of experiences. He knew how it felt to be well-cared-for as well as destitute. He knew how it felt to be successful and respected—and how it felt to be hated and scorned. He had experienced acceptance and rejection, joy and sorrow, encouragement and discouragement, and he had learned how to be *content* in the midst of every situation. In verse 12 he says he has learned the secret to contentment.

What do you think his secret is?

Let's look at some verses that will help us understand the secret to contentment. As you read them, note what they say.

1 Timothy 6:6 (page 912)

Hebrews 13:5 (page 928)

2 Corinthians 9:8 (page 886)

Isn't it interesting that each of these verses connect contentment with not focusing on wealth? But there are other causes of discontentment. Stop and think about it for a minute.

What causes discontentment in your life?

It is just a human tendency to look toward the material world to satisfy us rather than to God. It may seem more gratifying to go shopping or overeat than to go to Him. Paul had learned how to jump over that hurdle into a level of contentment that had nothing to do with his physical condition. He saw everything that happened to him as being filtered through God's loving fingers. Rather than resist the circumstance, he embraced God.

Contentment is the result of God working in you. It's looking to Him for satisfaction rather than anything or anyone else.

God's Strength in Our Weakness

Read Philippians 4:13 (page 901).

Paul relied completely on the strength of God to fulfill His plan for Paul's life. He relied on God's strength to endure the challenges he faced. God's strength was flowing through Paul, guarding his thoughts and impacting his behavior.

In 1 Timothy 1:12 (page 910), read Paul's words to Timothy, whom he had introduced at the beginning of his letter.

Can you describe a time when you felt God working in you,

enabling you to do something you know you couldn't have done on your own?

> God's strength is not visible, but the results of His strength working in us are visible, and those results will attract people to Jesus.
> The following verses tell us how we can access God's strength. As you read them note what they say.

Ephesians 3:16 (page 896)

Isaiah 40:31 (page 548)

Don't you love the imagery of that last verse? That is exactly what happens when we access the strength of God—it allows us to soar high above the circumstances that try to weigh us down. It infuses us with energy that comes straight from God Himself. It's wonderful to think about.

One of the best passages about the strength of God is 2 Corinthians 12:9-10 (page 888).

Do you see what this means? It isn't our strength that God works through, but rather our weakness! It's our weakness that best displays His power in us. And again we see the source of Paul's joy and contentment—it is the strength of God within him that continually overcomes all that he has endured. This is so important that I think we should stop right here and ask God to fill us with the truth of these verses and to help us really understand what this means for us.

Now read 2 Corinthians 4:7-10 (page 884).

Again we see the beauty of God's power when it shines through us, enabling us to survive *well* whatever happens. The following story is a beautiful illustration of this. An appraiser was examining some very old Indian clay pots. It turned out that they were ceremonial pots dating from about AD 1100. The stunning part of this story, however, is that the appraiser said that if the pots had been broken and pieced back together, they would have been worth triple the amount of money; this would have shown that the pots had been used for ceremonial purposes only and then cracked.

It doesn't matter how broken we are or how damaged we feel. God does not see us as useless. He lovingly pieces us back together, and we become more valuable than ever as a result of our brokenness— because He shines best through our brokenness. That is the incredible miracle of giving our lives to Jesus.

The Pleasure and Blessings of Giving

Read Philippians 4:14-16 (page 901).

What does this tell you about the Philippian church?

The Christians in Philippi had faithfully supported Paul since he first began his ministry in Europe, about ten years before the writing of this letter. Giving is an important part of being a follower of Jesus. Note what the following verses say:

Acts 20:35 (page 849)

2 Corinthians 8:5 (page 886)

2 Corinthians 9:7 (page 886)

Acts 11:28-30 (page 840)

2 Corinthians 8:12 (page 886)

Did you notice the first two passages had to do with giving of your time instead of money? Our time is also an important commodity.

What were the main thoughts you picked up from these passages about the money we give?

Our attitude about giving is even more important than the amount we give. Our heart and our motive is what matters most to God.
Read Philippians 4:17-18 (page 901).
Paul's pleasure in the gifts they have sent is based in his delight of how God will reward them. The thought gives him pleasure.

And how does this passage say God views our giving?

When you have given time, money, or other resources to God, have you ever considered the pleasure it gives God?

The Philippians were generous in their support of Paul—so much that he said he had more than he needed. By their support of him, they became a part of all that he did. They shared in the rewards of his work. It is the same when we give as directed by God to our church, missionaries, and worthy organizations. We share in the credit for what they are doing for Him. And He will bless us for it.

Read Philippians 4:19 (page 901).

How does Paul say God will reward us?

"All your needs." Not just our material needs but our physical, emotional, and spiritual needs as well. Since God knows us intimately and since He knows what tomorrow holds, we can absolutely trust Him with our needs. When our definition of *need* gets skewed, discontentment sets in because we're looking at our circumstances from a self-perspective and not a God-perspective. God has promised to take care of us. Period. If we do not have it, we do not need it.

Paul's Greetings and Final Prayer

Read Philippians 4:20-23 (page 901).

Paul closes his letter by praising God and sending greetings to and from various believers. What do you think about *"those in Caesar's household"* who also sent their greetings? Even in prison, Paul never missed an opportunity to tell people about Jesus—even some of the emperor's staff and government workers became believers as a result of his imprisonment.

Does knowing this inspire you to be bolder in telling others about Jesus? Have you been praying for the people you want to talk to, and has God given you an opportunity yet? Don't stop praying. Don't get discouraged. Their eternal life with Him is worth pursuing.

Paul's conclusion to his letter to the Philippians is similar to his introduction as he once again proclaims the grace of God. His words remind us that God's grace is the reason for our joy.

Verses 20 and 23 contain Paul's closing prayer of benediction and blessing to the Philippians. I think it would be wonderful to end this study by writing our own prayer of praise and blessing based on what God has shown us in this study of Philippians.

————— *Personal Reflection and Application* —————

From this chapter,

I see…

I believe…

I will…

Prayer

God, I give you all praise, the Father of my Lord Jesus Christ, who has blessed me with every spiritual blessing in the heavenly realms because I am united with Christ. Your unfailing love is better than life itself; how I praise you! I will praise you as long as I live, lifting up my hands to you in prayer. You satisfy me more than the richest feast. I will praise you with songs of joy (Ephesians 1:3, page 895, and Psalm 63:3-5, page 441).

Thoughts, Notes, and Prayer Requests

9

Joy in Practical Living

Review of Philippians 1–4

Note: This chapter is optional, but I think you'll find the discussion time well worth it. The questions from Philippians are designed to reinforce the principles for joyful living that we have talked about throughout this study.

It would be fun to combine the discussion time with a simple shared meal or snack. For example you could plan

- *a waffle breakfast with everyone bringing a fruit or favorite syrup topping*
- *a salad potluck*
- *a potato bake with everyone bringing a different topping*
- *a munchies potluck*
- *a cookie feast with everyone bringing their favorite cookies*

Have a fun, relaxing time of friendship, and let your discussion motivate each other toward the joy Jesus has for us.

As Seen On TV!" What comes to mind with those words? Ridiculous sales pitches? Shipping and handling prices greater than the item itself? The insidious power of persuasion?

How I wish I were with you, so I could see if you raise your hand in answer to this question: *Have you ever succumbed to their sales pitch?* I will sheepishly confess to having taken the bait a time or two. My all-time favorite gadget has been something called EZ-Moves. Oh my goodness! When I saw the advertisement I almost drooled. It promised that with the help of a 20-inch S-shaped bar for leverage and four small, slick plastic moving pads, I could move *anything* with no help at all.

It felt like a dream come true because I love rearranging my house. I immediately purchased an EZ-Moves and set to work. To my joy it lived up to its promise. I moved a heavy entertainment center without emptying one drawer or shelf or breaking a sweat. Grandfather clock? Moved! China cabinet? Moved! Are you ready for this? Hot tub? Moved! (I will note that it was empty at the time.) My husband and son stood by smirking—not lifting a finger to help—but then they didn't need to. (I know! I sound just like the people on TV.) This handy-dandy little gadget has opened up a whole new world for me where it seems nothing is impossible.

Not long after the hot tub move I was thinking about what an amazing thing leverage is. It extends your power far beyond your natural capabilities. Leverage is actually a great picture of what it means to have a relationship with God. When we commit our lives to Him, He becomes our leverage, enabling us to rise above debilitating circumstances, removing us from powerful temptations, and accomplishing what we didn't think was possible.

The most incredible thing He did for us, however, was when He leveraged the crushing weight of our sin through the blood of Jesus, allowing us to crawl out from under our old life and move into the freedom of a new life in Christ. While I will admit that my EZ-Moves does have limitations, God has none. There is no sin He can't remove, no pain He can't heal, and no life He can't redeem. With God, our ultimate leverage, nothing is impossible (Luke 1:37, page 780)!

─────── *Personal Reflection and Application* ───────

From this chapter,

I see...

I believe...

I will...

✤

Prayer

Lord God, you alone are my inheritance, my cup of blessing. You guard all that is mine. I will bless you who guides me; even at night my heart instructs me. I know you are always with me. I will not be shaken, for you are right beside me. No wonder my heart is glad, and I rejoice. My body rests in safety. You will show me the way of life, granting me the joy of your presence and the pleasures of living with you forever (Psalm 16:5,7-9,11, pages 419-420).

———— *Thoughts, Notes, and Prayer Requests* ————

_____

_____

_____

_____

_____

_____

_____

_____

_____

Discussion Questions

1. We've spent a lot of time during our study in learning about Paul's spiritual, physical, and emotional commitment to God. What characteristic of Paul's life has had the greatest impact on your life?

2. Paul was bold in sharing his faith and saw everything as an opportunity to share Jesus. How has his example motivated you to be bolder? Have you had an opportunity to talk about your faith since starting this study? Please share.

3. Paul issued some very challenging instructions on how we are to interact with others—the most challenging being to view others as more important than ourselves. How have those instructions changed your attitude or behavior?

4. In Philippians 2:14-16 (page 900) we are encouraged to shine for Christ. In today's culture, some Christians are not seen as shining examples. What can we personally do to change this and be more effective in influencing people toward Jesus?

5. The theme of Philippians is joy, and in chapter 3 Paul shows us how to have joy in all circumstances. What are some of the key instructions for achieving joy? Which one do you see to be the biggest challenge and why?

6. Philippians 3:12-14 (page 901) talks about the importance of putting the past behind us. In general there are three reasons we cannot let go of the past:

   • We cannot forgive what someone has done to us.

   • We cannot forgive ourselves for our own poor choices.

   • We cannot let go of circumstances that are beyond our control.

   How has our study of Philippians helped you to address any of these areas so that you can let go of the past?

7. Philippians 4:4-9 (page 901) gives practical (not to be confused with easy) instructions on how to experience unshakeable peace and joy. It also teaches us how to separate an attitude of contentment from our circumstances. Have you put any of these instructions to the test? What have been the results?

8. What has been your greatest takeaway from your study of Philippians?

9. What is your favorite verse from the book of Philippians?

Prayer

Lord, thank you for your commandments that are right and bring joy to my heart. Your commands are clear and give me insight for living. Help me to commit myself wholeheartedly to your words, keeping them as constant reminders. Give me courage to talk about them at home, at work, and all through my day. I will take refuge in you and rejoice; I will sing joyful praises forever. Spread your protection over me so that I, who love your name, may be filled with joy (Psalms 19:8, page 422; Deuteronomy 11:18-19, page 148; and Psalm 5:11, page 416).

Thoughts, Notes, and Prayer Requests

Journal Pages

Know God

It does not matter what has happened in your past. No matter what you've done, no matter how you've lived your life,

God is personally interested in you right now.
He cares about you.

God understands your frustration, your loneliness, your heartaches. He wants each of us to come to Him, to know Him personally.

God is so rich in mercy, and he loved us so much, that even
though we were dead because of our sins, he gave us
life when he raised Christ from the dead.
(It is only by God's grace that you have been saved!)
—Ephesians 2:4-5 (page 895)

God loves you.

He created you in His image. His desire is to be in relationship with you. He wants you to belong to Him.

Sadly, our sin gets in the way. It separates us from God, and without Him we are dead in our spirits. There is nothing we can do to close that gap. There is nothing we can do to give ourselves life. No matter how well we may behave.

But God loves us so much that He made a way to eliminate that gap and give us new life, His kind of life—to restore the relationship. His love for us is so great, so tremendous, that He sent Jesus Christ, His only Son, to earth to live, and then die—filling the gap and taking the punishment we deserve for refusing God's ways.

> God made Christ, who never sinned, to be the offering for our sin,
> so that we could be made right with God through Christ.
> —2 Corinthians 5:21 (page 884)

Jesus Christ, God's Son, not only died to pay the penalty for your sin, but He conquered death when He rose from the grave. He is ready to share His life with you.

Christ reconciles us to God. Jesus is alive today. He will give you a new beginning and a newly created life when you surrender control of your life to Him.

> Anyone who belongs to Christ has become a new person.
> The old life is gone; a new life has begun!
> —2 Corinthians 5:17 (page 884)

How do you begin this new life? You need to realize

> ...the necessity of repenting from sin and turning to God,
> and of having faith in our Lord Jesus.
> —Acts 20:21 (page 849)

Agree with God about your sins and believe that Jesus came to save you, that He is your Savior and Lord. Ask Him to lead your life.

God loved the world so much that he gave his one and only Son, so that everyone who believes in him will not perish but have eternal life. God sent his Son into the world not to judge the world, but to save the world through him.

—John 3:16-17 (page 811)

Pray something like this:

Jesus, I do believe you are the Son of God and that you died on the cross to pay the penalty for my sin. Forgive me. I turn away from my sin and choose to live a life that pleases you. Enter my life as my Savior and Lord.

I want to follow you and make you the leader of my life.

Thank you for your gift of eternal life and for the Holy Spirit, who has now come to live in me. I ask this in your name. Amen.

God puts His Spirit inside you, who enables you to live a life pleasing to Him. He gives you new life that will never die, that will last forever—eternally.

When you surrender your life to Jesus Christ, you are making the most important decision of your life. Stonecroft would like to offer you a free download of *A New Beginning*, a short Bible study that will help you as you begin your new life in Christ. Go to **stonecroft.org/ newbeginning**.

If you'd like to talk with someone right now about this prayer, call **1.888.NEED.HIM**.

Who Is Stonecroft?

Every day Stonecroft communicates the Gospel in meaningful ways. Whether side by side with a neighbor or new friend, or through a speaker sharing her transformational story, the Gospel of Jesus Christ goes forward. Through a variety of outreach activities and small group Bible studies specifically designed for those not familiar with God, and with online and print resources focused on evangelism, Stonecroft proclaims the Gospel of Jesus Christ to women where they are, as they are.

For more than 75 years, always with a foundation of prayer in reliance on God, Stonecroft volunteers have found ways to introduce women to Jesus Christ and train them to share His Good News with others.

Stonecroft understands and appreciates the influence of one woman's life. When you reach her, you touch everyone she knows—her family, friends, neighbors, and co-workers. The real Truth of the Gospel brings real redemption into real lives.

Our life-changing, faith-building community resources include:

- ***Stonecroft Bible and Book Studies***—both topical and chapter-by-chapter studies. We designed Stonecroft studies for those in small groups—those who know Christ and those who do not yet know Him—to simply yet profoundly discover God's Word together.

- ***Stonecroft Prays!***—calls small groups of women together to pray for God to show them avenues to reach women in their community with the Gospel.

- ***Outreach Events***—set the stage for women to hear and share the Gospel with their communities. Whether in a large venue, workshop, or small group setting, Stonecroft women find ways to share the love of Christ.

- ***Stonecroft Military***—a specialized effort to honor women connected to the U.S. military and share the Gospel with them while showing them the love of Christ.

- ***Small Group Studies for Christians***—these resources reveal God's heart for those who do not yet know Him. The Aware Series includes *Aware*, *Belong*, and *Call*.

- ***Stonecroft Life Publications***—clearly explain the Gospel through stories of people whose lives have been transformed by Jesus Christ.

- ***Stonecroft.org***—offers fresh content daily to equip and encourage you.

Dedicated and enthusiastic Stonecroft staff serve you via Divisional Field Directors stationed across the United States, and a Home Office team who support tens of thousands of dedicated volunteers worldwide.

Your life matters. Join us today to impact your communities with the Gospel of Jesus Christ. Become involved with Stonecroft.

STONECROFT

| Get started:
connections@stonecroft.org
800.525.8627 | Support Stonecroft:
stonecroft.org/donate | Order resources:
stonecroft.org/store
888.819.5218 |

Books for Further Study

DeMoss, Nancy Leigh. *Choosing Gratitude: Your Journey to Joy.* Chicago, IL: Moody Publisher, 2011.

George, Elizabeth. *Experiencing God's Peace.* Eugene, OR: Harvest House Publishers, 2000.

Ladd, Karol. *A Woman's Passionate Pursuit of God.* Eugene, OR: Harvest House Publishers, 2011.

Lewis, C.S. *Surprised by Joy.* San Diego, CA: Harcourt, Inc., 1955.

Lucado, Max. *Life Lessons: Philippians.* Nashville, TN: Thomas Nelson, 2007.

Ogilvie, Lloyd J. *Asking God Your Hardest Questions.* Colorado Springs, CO: Shaw Books, Waterbrook Press, 1996.

Warren, Kay. *Choose Joy.* Grand Rapids, MI: Revell Books, 2012.

Stonecroft Resources

Stonecroft Bible Studies make the Word of God accessible to everyone. These studies allow small groups to discover the adventure of a personal relationship with God and introduce others to God's unlimited love, grace, forgiveness, and power. To learn more, visit **stonecroft.org/biblestudies**.

Who Is Jesus? (6 chapters)

He was a rebel against the status quo. The religious community viewed Him as a threat. The helpless and outcast considered Him a friend. Explore the life and teachings of Jesus—this rebel with a cause who challenges us today to a life of radical faith.

What Is God Like? (6 chapters)

What is God like? Is He just a higher power? Has He created us and left us on our own? Where is He when things don't make sense? Discover what the Bible tells us about God and how we can know Him in a life-transforming way.

Who Is the Holy Spirit? (6 chapters)

Are you living up to the full life that God wants for you? Learn about the Holy Spirit, our Helper and power source for everyday living, who works in perfect harmony with God the Father and Jesus the Son.

Connecting with God (8 chapters)

Prayer is our heart-to-heart communication with our heavenly Father. This study examines the purpose, power, and elements of prayer, sharing biblical principles for effective prayer.

Today I Pray

When we bow before God on behalf of someone who doesn't yet know of His saving work, of His great love in sending His Son Jesus, of His mercy and goodness, we enter into a work that has eternal impact. Stonecroft designed *Today I Pray* as a 30-day intercessory prayer commitment that you may use to focus your prayers on behalf of a specific person, or to pray for many—because your prayers are powerful and important!

Prayer Worth Repeating (15 devotions)

There is no place where your prayers to the one and only God cannot penetrate, no circumstance prayers cannot impact. As the mother of adult children, your greatest influence into their lives is through prayer. *Prayer Worth Repeating* is a devotional prayer guide designed to focus your prayers and encourage you to trust God more deeply as He works in the lives of your adult children.

Pray & Play Devotional (12 devotions)

It's playgroup with a purpose! Plus Mom tips. For details on starting a Pray & Play group, visit **stonecroft.org/prayandplay** or call **800.525.8627**.

Prayer Journal

A practical resource to strengthen your prayer life, this booklet includes an introductory section about the importance of prayer, the basic elements of prayer, and a clear Gospel presentation, as well as 40 pages of journaling your prayer requests and God's answers.

Prayer—Talking with God

This booklet provides insight and biblical principles to help you establish a stronger, more effective prayer life.

Aware (5 lessons)

Making Jesus known every day starts when we are *Aware* of those around us. This dynamic Stonecroft Small Group Bible Study about "Always Watching and Responding with Encouragement" equips and engages people in the initial steps to the joys of evangelism.

Belong (6 lessons)

For many in today's culture, the desire to belong is often part of their journey to believe. *Belong* explores how we can follow in Jesus' footsteps—and walk with others on their journey to belong.

Call (7 lessons)

Every day we meet people without Christ. That is God's intention.

He wants His people to initiate and build friendships. He wants us together. *Call* helps us take a closer look at how God makes Himself known through our relationships with those around us.

Discover together God's clear calling for you and those near to you.

These and many more Stonecroft resources are available to you. Order today to impact your communities with the Gospel of Jesus Christ. Simply visit **stonecroft.org/store** to get started.

If you have been encouraged and brought closer to God by this study, please consider giving a gift to Stonecroft so that others can experience life change as well. You can find information about giving online at **stonecroft.org.** (Click on the "Donate" tab.)

If you'd like to give via telephone, please contact us at **800.525.8627**. Or you can mail your gift to

Stonecroft
10561 Barkley, Suite 500
Overland Park, KS 66212

STONECROFT

10561 Barkley, Suite 500, Overland Park, KS 66212
Telephone: 800.525.8627
E-mail: connections@stonecroft.org | stonecroft.org

Abundant Life Bible
New Living Translation
Holy Bible

*Experience the presence of God
in everyday life*

Stonecroft is pleased to partner with Tyndale to offer the New Living Translation Holy Bible as the companion for our newly released Stonecroft Bible Studies.

The New Living Translation translators set out to render the message of the original Scripture language texts into clear, contemporary English. In this *translation*, scholars kept the concerns of both formal-equivalence and dynamic-equivalence in mind. Their goal was a Bible that is faithful to the ancient texts and eminently readable. The result is a translation that is both accurate and powerful.

TRUTH MADE CLEAR

Features of the Abundant Life Bible

- Features are easy-to-use and written for people who don't yet know Jesus Christ personally.
- Unequaled clarity and accuracy
- Dictionary included
- Concordance included
- Old Testament included

- Introductory notes on important abundant life topics such as:
Gospel presentation	Practical guidance
Joy	Life's tough issues
Peace	Prayer
- Insights from a relationship with Jesus Christ.
- Ideal Scripture text for those not familiar with the Bible!

 Tyndale House Publishers

To order: stonecroft.org/store
888.819.5218